A Complete Guide to Sil

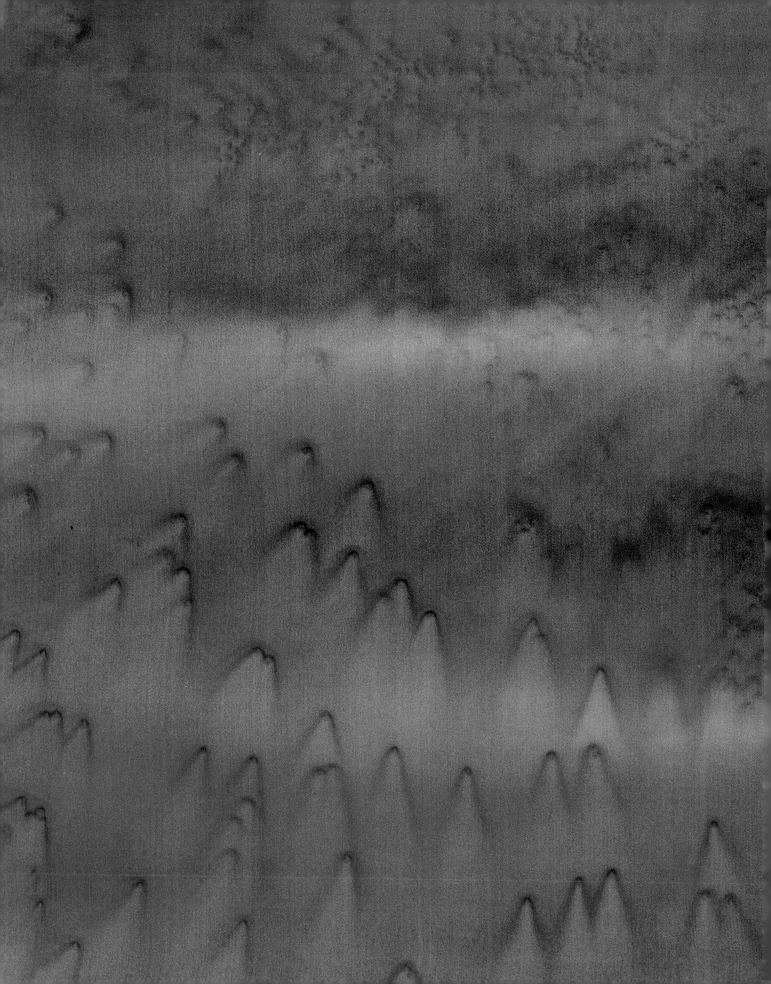

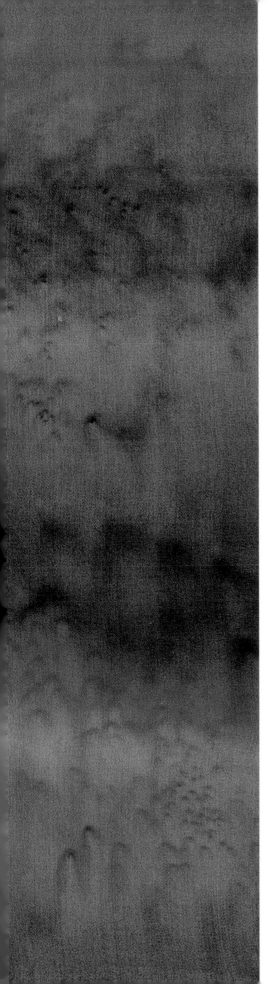

Susanne Hahn

A Complete Guide to
Silk Painting

Search Press

Contents

Introduction

Painting on silk is now an extremely popular art form and you can find a wide range of beautiful and exciting designs in high-class gift and fashion stores, or at most craft fairs. Items produced by these silk artists and craftspersons include not only such simple projects as brooches, scarves and greetings cards, but also cushions, wallhangings, pictures and even clothing, many of which can easily be reproduced by the enthusiastic amateur. The design possibilities are limitless, as no two paintings are ever exactly the same, however hard you may try to repeat a masterpiece!

As a result of all this interest, I am constantly asked for more information about this intriguing subject and this book has been based on my many years of painting on silk and teaching others the techniques. I have worked with children, housewives and students and I can therefore offer the beginner an easy-to-understand but comprehensive introduction to painting on silk. I also hope that more advanced students and teachers will find this book a treasure-trove of stimulating suggestions, either to use as an addition to set courses or lectures, or as a source of ideas which will benefit their own experiments. Obviously, such a subject, with origins reaching back over so many centuries, cannot be treated in depth in such limited space but I shall endeavor to make you aware of the basics, in the hope that you will be spurred on to discover more for yourself.

Painting on silk is almost as old as the discovery of silk as a fabric, so the book begins with a brief résumé of its historical background and then gives details of this incredible natural fibre, such as how it is obtained and processed. This is followed by a detailed account of the equipment and materials required for painting on silk and goes on to explain the various techniques and processes used. Each method described is illustrated with examples of the effects you can obtain, which will help you to understand and master different aspects of the craft. The following chapter provides a wealth of practical hints and instructions on making such items as wallhangings and lampshades. I can almost guarantee that everyone who begins to paint on silk will sooner or later want to create their own design; maybe a picture to enhance the decor of a room, a cushion as a gift for a friend, or something as simple as a brooch to highlight a favourite dress.

The book closes with a gallery of exciting contemporary creations by leading silk artists. At this point I would like to take the opportunity of thanking all those who helped me to produce this book: my family, without whose tolerance I could never have written it; my publishers, without whose assistance it would never have appeared and, most gratefully, all those artists who so generously made their work available to me.

Finally, I do hope that I will succeed in inspiring others with some small part of my own enthusiasm for the subject. Perhaps you, too, will find pleasure in exploring the art and craft which has fascinated me for so many years and which I still find wholly engrossing. To such a reader, I dedicate this book.

The history of painting on silk

Asian history

Any researcher into the origins of painting on silk will soon acknowledge the decisive Asian influence on the development of the technique. It can be traced back by means of a number of surviving pieces through the Sung Dynasty (AD 960–1278), and the Han period (BC 206–AD 220), into the literature of the Chou Dynasty (BC 1030–771). The latter period provides the first indications of painted silk banners.

It is not possible to consider the history of painting on silk separately from the traditions of Chinese and Japanese painting as a whole. Although paper was used as a

*Fan painting: **Hibiscus blossom with silkworm**. Ink and watercolour on silk. China, Sung Dynsasty 960–1127.*

medium much later than silk, both materials must stand side by side as equals in the phases of development, so that the same sizes, techniques and motifs may be found on both silk and paper backgrounds. Moreover, ideological changes and transformations in subject matter affected the entire spectrum of painting.

In looking at the history of this art form, particular attention must be paid to the differences between Chinese, Japanese and general European painting. This section deals with the major types of oriental pictures, such as horizontal and vertical scrolls, screens, fans and album leaves.

*Tai Wen-Chin: **Fisherman asleep in a boat**. Painting on silk, China c. 1446. The final effect does not depend on bright colours but on an interplay of understated areas and various graphic details.*

Horizontal scrolls

The horizontal, or long hand-scroll, is the oldest form of picture in China. Its counterpart in Japan is called a 'makimono', or 'rolled thing'. The scroll was placed horizontally on a table for viewing and it developed from the ancient Chinese form of a book; a roll of silk or paper.

The system of reading in horizontal lines from right to left was translated into terms suitable to the contemplation of a picture, so that at any one time it was possible to observe a 70–100cm (28–40in) broad section of a scroll several metres (yards) in length, while the rest remained rolled up. The picture itself unrolled like a seamless narrative over the whole length of the scroll. It was often bordered with a patterned edge of matching colour in silk or paper and was fastened to a wooden spindle for storage.

Hanging scrolls

The hanging scroll has developed from the ancient form of devotional image, which was probably already in use in the third century BC as a 'magical picture'. In Japan this is called a 'kakemono' or 'hanging thing'.

The subject matter of these sometimes small vertical pictures was often a single main figure, which was enclosed in a framework of ribbons and other decorations. Initially, the hanging scroll was reserved exclusively for religious (Buddhist) use, but from the eighth century AD it was also adopted by Chinese painters and, eventually, came to occupy a position in its own right alongside the hand-scroll.

The height and width of the painted surface was variable and could be made from silk as well as paper. It could also serve as a support for a mounted fan. Unlike modern mounts, the pastel-coloured brocade strips placed round the edges of the painted silk featured dragon and phoenix designs, especially along both sides.

*Ma-1: **Two parrots on a blossoming peach tree**. Natural colours on silk. Signed, with collector's stamp at lower left-hand edge. China, Ming Dynasty 1368–1644. Size, 165.5 × 79.5cm (65 × 31in).*

Kano Tanigosu (1702–1774): **Senin Tekai with a crooked stick and the gourd bottle on his back, exhales his soul.** *This taoist hermit, one of the 'eight immortals', is depicted sending his spiritual self to be counselled by Lao Tse in heaven. Ink on silk, Japan 1773.*
Size, 99 × 44.5cm (39 × 17½ in).

Chinese scroll: **Scene from a Taoist legend.** *Ink and heightened wash on silk, showing two celestial guardians and several divinities, 17th–18th century.*
Size, 108 × 54cm (42½ × 21in).

Album leaves

The album leaf is a transitional form between the scroll and the book. As a far-eastern art form, its height is equivalent to that of the horizontal scroll and its width varies in accordance with the theme and the artistic design.

Several leaves would be gathered into an album of 8 to 24 pages and the album would be stored in a specially prepared fabric container, or a box made of card and covered with brocade. An album might be made up from the work of one or more artists, and the subject matter consist of different topics, or variations on a single theme.

Fans

The fan was the essential accessory of a cultured person and a possession which was carried everywhere. Friendly visits and special occasions were excuses for decorating fans, or inscribing them with verses. Very often, gifted amateurs produced exquisite fans.

The originally round, or trapezoid silk or paper shape with rounded corners, changed to the now familiar and more convenient folding fan. As silk tends to fray with age and use, most surviving fans are made from paper, which has a much longer life.

Screens

The screen was generally the largest format used for Chinese and Japanese painting. Screen-painting flourished in sixteenth century Japan, where the technique was still further developed. It had many uses, as it was portable and it could be erected and displayed as required in different parts of a dwelling, thus fulfilling both architectural and decorative functions. It could also serve as a room-divider, a wall, and a place or concealment. Of course, authentic calligraphers and artists did not approve of this art form, as its very functionalism was inimical to their refined aesthetic sensibility. This led to a tendency to decorate the panels

Mori Sosen (1749–1821): **Two monkeys on a branch.** *Japanese, scroll painting on silk.*

with carvings, marquetry or lacquered designs, instead of painting.

In China the 'liberal' arts of calligraphy, painting, poetry and music are still carefully distinguished from the 'applied' arts, more associated with the artisan. The latter can be determined by workshop production, extremely high material costs and a vast expenditure of time. Dexterity and experience also characterized the craftsman's ability, whereas the practitioner of the 'fine' arts would have decided intellectually on every brushstroke spiritually in advance.

The present-day Chinese and Japanese attitude to art and artists remains quite different to that of Europe. For the most part, pictures and scrolls are stored in specially manufactured and, very often, appropriately decorated wooden cases. On each occasion, therefore, works of art have to be removed for display, whether in honour of an appreciative visitor, or on special seasonal or religious festivals. Their contemplation is a traditional ceremony and a spiritual complement to the art of painting. To western eyes, a greater significance is therefore ascribed in Asia to the creative process itself rather than the actual painting which is produced.

The topics depicted were, for the most part, wholly imaginative but myths and mythical figures played a large part in the design. Still lifes, portraits or scenes of everyday life, which have long been self-sufficient themes in western art, were therefore not known in China for several centuries. Religious subjects were the only other ones which were thought to be worthy of artistic treatment.

Eventually the choice of subject matter developed as traditions changed and for a long time, figure painting was the dominant theme. Plants and animals were used to decorate screens and wallhangings and such motifs formed the central theme of the picture, never being dominated by the merely suggested background. Plants and animals also became associated with a variety of symbols and allegories; for instance, bamboo, plum blossom, cranes and turtles all represent a long life.

Landscape became a pictorial theme in its own right much earlier in China than in the west. The Chinese saw themselves as part of nature and the fourth century saw the development of nature poetry, and the fifth century, that of landscape painting. Nature is often represented as a vast, hieratic whole in which mountains, water and plants merge as a single overall entity. In painting these subjects there was often no attempt to achieve depth or perspective by means of a horizon dividing heaven and earth into two separate areas. Everything existed together as a single

Details from a 6m (5½ yd) long scroll painting on silk. A royal hunting party, showing a tent with dancers and concubines. China, c.1700.

whole and, very often, the human figure was protrayed as a minute subject in this natural oneness.

Until the fifth century BC, a written representation was the preferred, precisely stylized and simplified form of painting in Asia. The image and script worked as a whole and, to some extent, were used together to define an exact meaning. In the second century BC, the written word was used for the first time on its own for secular and organizational tasks, and the way was paved for the separation of script and the painted image. We must remember, however, that even today writing is not considered merely as a form of communication and in calligraphy, which is the art of fine writing, a very high value is placed on the form of script and on the very process of writing.

Paper has only been known since the second century AD and it was originally made in Asia from scraps of silk and other plant fibres. Even in the third century AD it was rare and expensive but gradually came to be used more and more because, in the long run, it proved longer lasting than silk, which frayed with time. It was also possible to paint and write more directly on to paper, which meant that ink, already in use before the Han period of BC 206 to 220 AD, became increasingly more important. As the quality of brushes also began to improve at this time, there was a considerable upsurge of interest in the complementary arts of writing and painting.

One obvious reason for the close association between writing and painting in Asia was, and continues to be, their use of the same materials; ink, silk and paper. The brush is the universal tool for painting and writing and its flexible tuft has a relatively firm core, enclosed in longer external hairs with fine ends. The tuft is firmly fixed into the end of a bamboo tube and as soon as the hairs are moistened, they come to a fine point. This is an essential prerequisite both for delicate, sensitive writing and for the artist's more generous strokes. The correct position of the brush and the movements of the hand require much practice and years of experience. The criteria for lively and versatile lines, whether in caligraphy or art, are precision, rhythm and broad and fine brushstrokes.

The most important means of expression is black ink. An ink block is still made from soot and bone glue, and it is sufficient merely to rub the moistened block on a grinding-stone to obtain the minimal amount needed for writing and painting. The ratio of soot to water, and the flow of the brush, determine the light and dark effects of the brushstrokes. The tonality obtained, ranges from the most delicate grey to the deepest black and offers endless possibilities for background washes and monochrome painting.

Colours, on the other hand, very often play a quite subordinate role in Chinese and Japanese painting. They consist, for the most part, of natural water-soluble pigments, either animal, mineral or vegetable substances and a binding agent. The pigment could be metallic oxide soils, pollen, or an extract of roots, barks and leaves. Like black ink-blocks, coloured paints also have to be ground on a stone and water must be added to give the required consistency. In the painting process, shapes and figures are sketched out first in ink, then filled in with colour and, finally, the contours are re-emphasized. The largely transparent colours obtained mean that a design must be decided in advance in every detail, and requires absolute concentration while painting. Since it is extremely difficult to make any corrections, to some extent the process of painting itself assumes more importance

Painting on silk. Unknown Japanese painter, early 19th century: Lady in a winter morning setting, wearing a richly decorated outer robe and a white shawl over a fire-red kimono.

*Embroidered silk: **Boy on a water buffalo**. This embroidery tries to imitate the basic elements of a painting, with gentle transitions from light to dark. Calligraphy on left. China, 18th–19th century. Size, 26.5 × 37cm (10½ × 14½ in).*

Kosode, or standard-sized kimono. A short-sleeved theatrical robe in white silk with gold embroidery and painting, which is unique. In contrast to the richly coloured embroidery, the painting depends largely on graphic elements, with an emphasis on the interplay of lines and various shades of grey. Japan. 18th century.

Lady with a large fan, gladioli and a Pekinese. Painted on silk by an unknown artist. Japan, early 19th century.

than the result. Moreoever, the structure of handmade paper, which is something like blotting paper, immediately soaks up and retains ink and paint, thus compelling the painter to work rapidly and accurately.

Paint is more versatile on silk, as it can be dispersed, restarted, moved about and even partially removed. It was not until the mid-seventeenth century, however, that the Japanese fan-painter, Miyazaki Yuzensai, from Kyoto province, invented a hitherto unknown colouring method, the 'Yuzen' technique. This enabled him to sketch any design on to the material by first applying a paste made from rice-glue and bran with a stick. Once the paste was dry, the material was coloured and the paste subsequently washed out. As with present-day batik or gutta techniques in silk painting, the areas covered with paste remained resistant to paint. This new way of designing on silk became especially useful for painting kimonos. Embroiderers would sometimes try to imitate this wonderful painting technique, and special care was taken with fine embroidery, using different threads, to achieve delicate chiaroscuro effects. This technique gives an almost sculptured effect to designs depending on light and dark patterning, and the embroidery on page 13 is an example of this process.

Europe

Just as silk from Asia enriched our western world, so oriental painting provided us with design ideas and inspiration. The constant expansion of world trade and voyages of discovery to other lands had an enormous influence on our environment, interior decoration, fashion and the entire life style in Europe. However, the actual examples of oriental art, such as horizontal and hand scrolls, album leaves and screens were not adopted.

The one item from the Asian repertoire which was very fashionable for a time was the fan, as is evident from the number of European locations where it became quite the rage. At first its use spread largely in the form of the 'uchiwa', or round fan on a straight handle, which became increasingly popular as a coveted accessory in fourteenth and fifteenth century Europe. Towards the end of the sixteenth century, it was replaced by a new form of fan imported from Japan, the folding fan, which is also our present-day notion of a 'typical' fan.

Strict rules, technical manuals, and even the formation of a guild governed the painting of fan leaves, which were then mounted on artistically decorated frames, very often made from ivory or tortoiseshell. From 1860 to early in the present century, the trade in fans became a virtual flood and a variety

Painting on silk: section of a wall covering from the palace of the young Frederick the Great. France, 1736–1740.

of inexpensive imports from Japan found their way into many fashionable wardrobes.

The oriental influence became especially strong after the Japanese contribution to the World Exhibition in Paris in 1878. Edgar Degas was one of several artists who produced a considerable number of works in this genre and Denis, de Fleure, Gauguin, Kokoschka, de Nittis and Signac

also painted fan leaves. They were often used to convey very personal emotions and thoughts to the female friends for whom they were intended. These paintings were executed on paper and silk and not only gouache, but watercolour, tempera and oils were used. Georges de Fleure even resorted to lithography for his fan leaves. When using these traditional paints and techniques, however, there

seemed no way of avoiding the tightening of the silk, which resulted in partial loss of sheen and transparency, although this was not so important when the fan was used as a form of wall decoration.

In the industry generally, as well as in the production of fans, France played, and continues to play, a major role in the manufacture and weaving of silk in Europe. That is probably the main reason why the French chemical industry was one of the first to try to develop paints which were more appropriate to modern silk painting requirements, and many of the paints now available originated in France. These firms specialize in the manufacture of brilliantly coloured, steam-fixed paints, see page 33. Today, experiments continue to develop new products and methods which will make the fixing and preservation of painted silk fabrics an easier process, while still retaining the brilliance and suppleness which this technique can produce.

As more and more techniques are explored, new mediums are also becoming available to the avid painter. You could try experimenting with a background of pure cotton, as well as blends of silk and man-made fibres. These do not produce such fluid and lustrous results as painted silk but they are certainly worth considering, particularly in terms of cost.

△ Edgar Degas (1834–1917): **Ballet dancers behind the scenes.**
Fan painting in gouache on silk, laid down on cardboard and
delicately heightened with gold. Paris, c. 1879.
Size 31 × 61cm (12¼ × 24in).
Kormfeld & Klipstein, Berne.

◁ Folding fan with nasturtium motif, painted on silk. Germany,
c. 1890–1900.

Paul Signac (1863–1935): **The Seine near Herblay.** Oils on silk.
Size, 31.5 × 68.5cm (12½ × 27in).
Pontoise Museums, (Tabet and Pissaro).

Silk
A natural material

The discovery of silk

The word 'silk' brings many different word associations to mind; priceless, lustrous, luxurious, Asia, the Silk Roads, ancient trading methods, and so on. Because of its long history, these terms are appropriate, but even more so when we understand how much effort is required to manufacture silk, especially in past centuries, and realize that silk yarns and fabrics were not always so readily available, or at such low costs as today.

Silk can be traced back to Asia and to the highly developed civilization of ancient China, and as far back as 3000 BC there is evidence of the rearing of silkworm. Because of its beauty and rarity, the gold rate for silk was exceptionally high and, in present-day terms, a kilo (2¼ lb) of crimson silk would cost about £1300 sterling.

Silk reached Europe by means of the 10,000km (6210 mile) long silk roads, and each journey took between 6 and 8 years. Caravans had always carried various goods along these routes from at least the second century BC. The silk route extended from China, through central Asia to India and into Syria, which was part of the Roman empire. From there, sea routes led to Rome itself. However, cultural exchanges were not very extensive.

In addition to glass products precious stones and spices, spun and woven silk were the most desirable commodity in Europe and were exchanged for wine, resin, honey almonds, copper, tin and wool. Because of the secrecy surrounding the fabric, there was uncertainty about the origins of silk and its composition. Death was the penalty for betraying the secrets of silk manufacture, or for exporting silkworms, mulberry seeds or anything to do with the process. In this way China protected its silk monopoly for two thousand years.

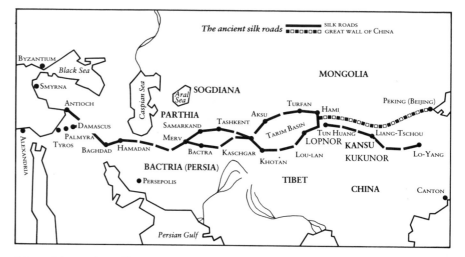

Map of the ancient silk routes.

Chronology	Development of silk industry
BC	
3000	First mention of silkworm rearing in China
3000–2000	Confucius mentions silkworms and mulberry trees
2000	Preparation of a 'silk calendar'; the life of the silkworm is the measure for the everyday life of the Chinese
200	Silk as a precious commodity passes along the silk routes to the countries of the known civilized world; until then silk was a monopoly of the Chinese; silk smuggled to Korea
AD	
3rd–5th centuries	Silk reaches Japan and countries next to China
6th century	552 AD; two monks bring silkworm eggs, mulberry branches and details of silkworm culture to Byzantium
7th century	After conquering the Persians, the Arabs take up the cultivation of silk and during their campaigns introduce it to North Africa, southern Spain and Sicily
13th–14th centuries	Italy and France become the foremost European silk cultivators and manufacturers; improved weaving techniques; Lyons a centre of the silk industry
17th century	Silk industry in Switzerland, Germany and Britain
18–20th centuries	Increasing industrialization and climatic variations in Europe, bring about the return of silk manufacture to its original location and to Japan, Korea and India; many European centres continue to process silk

In this setting trade is inconceivable without caravans.

A fragment of painted wallpaper showing how silk was dyed

As silk became increasingly important for Chinese trade with the western world, their trading partners became more covetous. The wildest rumours and myths circulated regarding silk production, and it was said that it came from the leaves of a tree, or from Chinese desert flowers. According to one of these legends, the Chinese Empress Hsi-Ling Shi, (who is still honoured as the goddess Yuanfei, the patron of silk), was in her palace garden one day and happened to notice the 'fruits' of the mulberry tree moving. On closer inspection, she observed that they were not fruits, but silkworms spinning fine threads which had a unique sheen. Other sources say that when the Empress was breakfasting beneath a mulberry tree, something plopped into her tea and then dissolved into separate threads. Female sagacity led her to collect these items together for later use!

In the second century BC, refugees brought information about silk production to Korea, from whence it finally reached Japan in AD 200. Several ambassadors to China had repeatedly asked the current ruler for the secret of silk manufacture, but without success; all they managed to obtain was the increased vigilance of customs men checking anyone leaving the country. Possibly out of revenge, the King of Khotan asked for the hand of a princess of the imperial house of China, solely in order to persuade her to bring mulberry seeds and silkworm cocoons with her.

In AD 552 the Roman Emperor of the East, Justinian (483–565), ordered two Byzantine monks to carry out a spying mission, in order to discover how silkworms were reared and cared for, and details of the manufacture and processing of the fibres. They brought silkworm eggs in their hollow pilgrim staffs from Khotan to Europe.

In the middle of the seventh century, the Arabs introduced silk to the Mediterranean area, as far as Spain and Italy. In the fifteenth century, at the instigation of Louis XI (1423–1483), the French silk industry far outclassed the rest of Europe. An improvement in weaving techniques allowed the production of larger quantities and also rationalized working procedure, and Lyons became an important silk centre. As early as the fourteenth century the German silk trade flourished in Augsburg, Nuremberg, Ulm and Regensburg. The Prussian silk industry prospered under Frederick the Great (1712–1786), towards the end of the eighteenth century, but not for long.

To bring the story up to date, it was only between 1934 and 1945 that Germany once again promoted silk manufacture as being of prime importance, when parachute silk was in urgent demand. The manufacture of silk in Europe nowadays is insignificant, but small quantities are produced at Lullingstone Silk Farm, near Sevenoaks in Kent, and it has become a tradition for English silk to be incorporated into wedding dresses for the British Royal Family.

Silkworms

Silk is actually produced by creatures which spin a thread and then use it for various purposes, and silkworms are not the only instance of this practice. For example, there is a Mediterranean shellfish, (*pinna squamosa*), which uses fine thread to adhere itself to the sea-bed. In ancient times this 'sea-silk', (*byssus*), was used for very precious garments and stockings and even today, in some parts of southern Italy it is used to make netting, tapestries and fabrics. Then there is the thread of the garden or cross-spider, (*aranea diadema*), which for a long time was an essential component in the manufacture of optical instruments for nautical navigation.

Wheel-net spiders, (*nephila*), can catch birds in their 1–2m (1–2yd) diameter webs, without severe damage to the webs, yet the filaments are so fine that 18,000 threads together would be needed to match the thickness of ordinary sewing thread. A verse in Isaiah, (59:6), could well refer to these incredible structures: 'Their webs shall not become garments, neither shall they cover themselves with their works'. Even today, the most up-to-date forms of industrial processing can make no profitable use of them. In Madagascar there were attempts to raise these spiders, but a major problem in rearing them was their dependence on live prey. This made them difficult to keep in great numbers, as the expenditure exceeded the profit.

Many ants, millipedes and even some butterflies and moths, shortly before the third stage of metamorphosis from egg-caterpillar-cocoon-pupa-insect, try to protect themselves from enemies and the weather by wrapping themselves in so many twists of silken thread that they end up in a secure cocoon. Thus protected, they develop without disturbance, only to leave the cocoon when the transformation is at an end and they can look after themselves.

The silk used nowadays for silk painting is a thread of this kind, produced by the mulberry moth, (*bombyx mori*), whose cocoons provide the largest quantity and highest quality of thread. Altogether, silk provides about 1.5% of the world's total natural fibre production. Silk fibres, however, are often mixed with other types of thread, but in accordance with the textile law and trade descriptions legislation in many countries, the proportions of mixture must be stated. Natural silk is obtainable in many different qualities, as a result not only of the methods of spinning and weaving employed, but of the various types of silkworm and the texture of the raw material produced by different diets. In general, a distinction is made between the silk of the mulberry silkworm and that of the various wild silkworms, (*saturnides*), which have also been domesticated. Because of this, as with any other natural fibre, no two pieces of silk will be identical.

Silkworms (bombyx mori).

A silkworm wrapping itself in a cocoon.

A silk cocoon hanging in the branches.

A silkworm before pupation.

A silkworm pupa in the cocoon.

The silkworm moth emerges.

Mulberry silk

Raw mulberry silk has been produced for centuries by a system of breeding and processing cocoons, and is referred to as 'synthetic' silk. As you would expect, the caterpillars of the moth are fed almost exclusively on the leaves of the mulberry tree, (*morus alba*). The mulberry silkworm moth is a small, yellowish-white, inconspicuous insect and has become so highly domesticated that mass production is no longer a problem. Unfortunately, as a result of this, and despite having fully formed wings, they have lost the ability to fly and so remain captive.

Immediately after fertilization the female moth lays approximately 500 oval eggs, about 1mm (1/16 in) long, and then she dies. The lifespan of the male is also just as short, only 2 to 4 days, and both sexes exist purely for reproduction. The eggs are flat and white to begin with, becoming bluish-violet in colour, and then grey. After about 10 to 12 days at the correct air temperature and humidity, they hatch out.

The tiny caterpillars are no more then 3mm (1/8 in) long and immediately begin eating huge amounts of fresh mulberry leaves. At first they eat only the young, tender tips of the leaves but, later on, whole stems and twigs are consumed. After about 35 days, towards the end of their life as a caterpillar, they are about as thick as a finger and 8–9cm (3¼–3½ in) long. They will have eaten 7000–9000 times their original weight when hatched, and now weigh almost 4gm (1/8 oz). Their skin will have been shed four times during this terrific growth, because the outer skin does not grow with them.

Shortly before pupation, the fully-grown caterpillar stops eating and does not eat any food during the subsequent stages of development. By this time it has built up enough juice in its body to spin its cocoon. To begin this process, it secures itself to a bare forked twig and spins fluffy silk threads to provide a framework in which to build its cocoon. Moving its

A production team engaged in silk caterpillar breeding. Traditional painting by Commune member, Chao Huiro, born 1954. Watercolour on silk, 1976. Size, 59 × 44cm (23¼ × 17¼ in).

body in a figure of eight, the caterpillar wraps seemingly endless double threads around itself. These are squeezed out from the pair of glands running the length of its body and emitted through an opening at the top of its head. The emission from each gland remains separate but they are bound together by a protein called sericin, which hardens more slowly than the silk itself, so holding the cocoon together. The caterpillar wraps the threads around itself more than one million times, and in doing so loses about half its bodyweight.

After 2–3 days of exhausting work, the silk shell is finished and hangs like a ball of cottonwool from the bare twig. Inside, cut off from the world, the caterpillar pupates, and slowly develops into a moth. This can take up to 18 days and at the end of this period the moth secretes a brownish solution, containing enzymes which dissolve the sericin, allowing it to push its way through the texture of the cocoon. As soon as it is free the moth sets off in search of a mate, and then the whole cycle begins again.

In the manufacture of 'synthetic' silk, the moth is not allowed to complete this cycle, as if it did emerge from the cocoon, it would break the continuous filament and damage the thread. Only the best cocoons are selected for breeding and allowed to complete the full cycle. Most of the caterpillars are killed in their cocoons after a period of 12 days, using hot air or steam, or chemical processes.

To obtain the silk thread, the cocoons are first loosened in a warm leaching solution, at a temperature of 50°C (125°F). Brushes are used to slough off the rough outer layer of the cocoon, so that the valuable inner threads can be extracted. As the glue, or sericin, is separated from the actual silk substance, the bast, or outer fibrous layer, is slowly removed. Seven or eight of the cleaned cocoon threads are then gathered together to make the raw silk thread, and lightly twisted. The remaining sericin dries as soon as it leaves the hot water and as it hardens, it binds the threads into one.

To give you some idea of the

quantity of cocoons it would take to make a silk garment, about 5000 caterpillars will hatch out of 6gm (³/₁₆ oz) of eggs and they will produce between 10–11kg (22–24¼ lb) of fresh cocoons. As these dry, they lose about two-thirds of their weight, so that approximately 4kg (8¾ lb) of dry cocoons are left. The pure silk obtained from these will weigh about 1kg (2¼ lb), and a good quality silk

Mulberry tree plantation.

dress would weigh 400g (14oz) – which means that some 3000 cocoons will have been used to produce it!

Wild silk

With a wingspan of up to 28cm (11in), the wild silk moth is one of the largest insects on earth. Unlike the mulberry moth, they eat the leaves of a variety of deciduous trees. The term 'wild silk', however, is no longer strictly valid, as it dates from the time when the cocoons of this moth, which did not live in captivity, were collected out in the open after they had hatched. They are now semi-cultivated and, like the mulberry moth, are bred close to human habitations.

Wild silk has a rough, uneven thread structure, which is attributed to the relatively large proportion of

bast which it contains, see the diagram on page 23. This is readily accepted as it gives the silk a natural, or rustic quality and is even highly valued in the fashion trade.

The development from egg to cocoon takes about 30–70 days. Depending on the species, the cocoon is about 5cm (2in) long and 3cm (1¼ in) across. It is made up of 1000–2000 individual threads, which makes it impossible to unwind it in one operation and also means that it is unnecessary to kill off the insect before it hatches. All the moths, therefore, can be used for breeding and in this way many generations of 'crops' can be produced in a year.

Originally, wild silk was spun by hand straight from the cocoon, but nowadays, the mass of individual threads is processed into spun silk, after the removal of the sericin. As the sericin cannot be completely removed, wild silk always has a light tint and a certain amount of stiffness. Because of this, it is difficult to paint and cannot be worked with as easily as mulberry silk.

The best-known wild silks come from the Indian tussore moths (*antheraea mylitta*), the Chinese tussore moths (*antheraea perjyi*) – also called the 'oak moth', because it feeds on oak leaves – and from the Japanese tussore moths (*antheraea yamamai*), to produce Yamamai silk.

Tussore silk is also known as Honan or Shantung silk, and also, erroneously, as bast or raw silk. Shantung silk was named after the centre of the Chinese tussore moth industry, the Province of Shantung but the material called Honan silk is only half wild silk: the warp threads are mulberry silk and the weft, wild silk. Because of this it is smoother and finer than Shantung silk.

Less significant wild silks include Fagara and Anaphne, which are found in Africa, and Eri silk which is spun from the cocoons of the Eri moth in India.

Silk caterpillars, (bombyx mori) *on mulberry leaves.*

Silk fibres

As explained in the previous chapter, silk is a natural fibre produced by a variety of creatures. It is the longest naturally produced fibre, consisting mainly of proteins (albumen), and its most striking characteristics are its extraordinary glossiness and suppleness.

Of all the textile fibres, synthetic silk it is the one most like human skin in organic composition, and it has a similar tolerance. It has excellent insulation properties against both heat and cold, and it is able to absorb dampness of up to 30% of its dry weight, without actually feeling wet. Because of this, it has a regulating effect on the skin and does not restrict

The ends of the thread have to be found so that the silk can be unwound from the cocoons.

the skin from breathing. It is also resistant to attacks from moths and to rotting, but is sensitive to sunlight and alkaline substances. It has remarkable strength when both dry or wet. It can stretch by 15%, which means that a 1m (1yd) long silk thread can be stretched by up to 15cm (6in) without breaking.

The diagram on the left shows the exact composition of the fibre. A raw silk thread consists of about 76% fibre (silk substance); 22% sericin (bast); 1% fats (waxes and resins) and 1% pigments (minerals). Raw silk refers to the silk before the bast has been removed, consisting mainly of two fibrous threads, the actual silk substance. When the thread is being spun it is coated with bast, a glue-like substance, just before it comes out of the moth's spinning gland next to the mouth, and is stuck to another similar thread. Whereas the silk substance itself begins to harden immediately on contact with the air, the sericin, which dries more slowly, sticks the threads to the cocoon.

The colouration of the cocoon, and the subsequent shade of the raw silk, depends on the pigmentation that the caterpillar consumes with its food. The natural colourings and minerals settle in the sericin, but when the bast is removed from the silk, some of these are lost. After the leaching process in a 1–2% soap solution, only the light silk threads remain, which often weigh up to 30% less than the raw silk. This sharp drop in weight also means large financial losses, for which the producers sometimes try to compensate by weighting the threads with metallic or plant materials, often during the dyeing process. Using this trick can bring the weight up to four times that of the original raw silk. The disadvantages are that silk, heavily weighted in this way, becomes brittle more quickly, or deteriorates through oxidation.

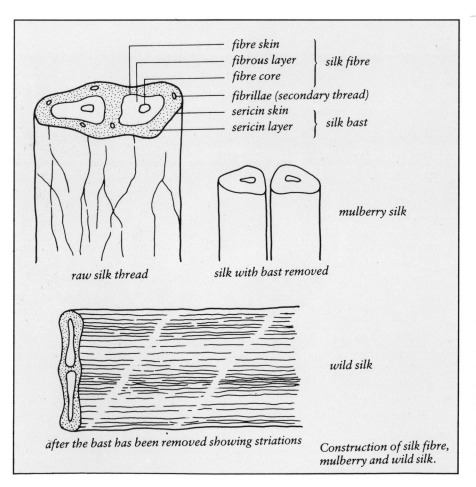

fibre skin
fibrous layer } silk fibre
fibre core
fibrillae (secondary thread)
sericin skin
sericin layer } silk bast

raw silk thread

mulberry silk

silk with bast removed

wild silk

after the bast has been removed showing striations

Construction of silk fibre, mulberry and wild silk.

The following list gives some of the processes applied to raw silk:-

Unbleached silk: Hard silk or bast silk; not leached; raw silk with no gloss which retains some bast, either yellow in colour (yellow bast), or white (white bast).

Supple silk: Matt silk; half the bast removed (sometimes called demi-cuite); softened silk with a weight reduction of 6 to 12%.

Silk with bast removed: Glossy silk, called 'cuite' silk; all of the bast removed; very soft with a weight reduction of 18 to 22% for Chinese and Japanese silk, or 25 to 30% for European quality.

Silk treated with weak acid: Sometimes referred to as 'avivierte' silk; when treated with a weak solution of acid has a crinkly feel.

Attempts to reproduce the qualities of natural silk by artificial means have not, so far, been very successful. The names given to artificial fibres which were previously used exclusively for pure silk, such as Crêpe de Chine or Crêpe Georgette, have blurred the differences between the two fabrics and confused the consumer. When buying silk, therefore, you should place less importance on the name itself and look for the internationally accepted symbol that is issued by the European Commission for Silk at Lyons, and guarantees 100% pure silk. The distinctive 'S' symbol stands for Silk, Seide, Soie or Seta, in the respective European languages.

The silk thread is checked.

The symbol that guarantees 100% pure silk.

From fibre to fabric

After extracting the raw silk from the cocoons, the next process is to spin it into silk threads which form the basis of all silk fabrics, some of which are not really suitable for the silk painter. The methods vary considerably, as to keep costs down it is necessary to use as much raw silk as possible, both from the cocoons of the mulberry moth which are in good condition, and those from the wild silk moths which are damaged.

Spool silk

This is the term used for a silk thread which has been unwound in one piece from the cocoon of the mulberry moth. To produce the thread, 7 or 8 strands are lightly twisted together to form the raw thread. Stronger twisting gives a thread referred to as 'poile', and very tight twisting results in a crêpe thread.

Spun silk

If the caterpillars have hatched from the cocoons, then the silk can no longer be unwound in one length. To produce this thread, pieces of fibre from mulberry silk cocoons and wild silk cocoons, from 5 to 25cm (2 to 9¾ in) long are spun together. Pieces of cocoons that cannot be unwound, matted silk, or fibres discarded from earlier processes are not used.

Noil silk

This is produced from fibres that are discarded from the spun silk process, with a length of only 1–5cm (½– 2in). The silk loses much of its brilliance in production and is used largely as a mixture with other fibres.

Organzine silk

This is a very hard-wearing thread, made from twisted raw threads of the highest quality and used as warp threads in weaving, or for knitted fabrics. Two threads are each twisted separately, then combined together in a reverse twist. There are 4 types of twist; organzine, voile, grenadine and crêpe.

Tram silk

This is the term used for untwisted, or

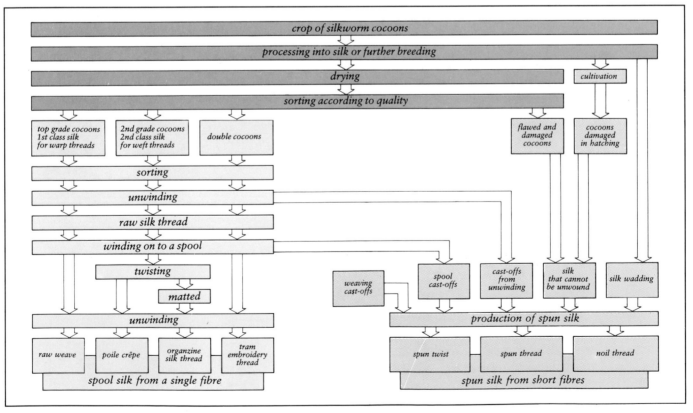

Production of silk threads – from cocoon to thread.

lightly twisted threads and is used as weft threads in weaving, or as embroidery silk.

Grenadine silk

This is produced from highly-twisted organzine threads.

Facts about silk fabrics

The quality of a silk fabric depends not only on the fibres and processing but, also, on the methods of weaving. As a guide to the table on page 28, which lists the different types of silk fabrics, it will help if you have some idea of the basic technique.

The actual weaving process governs the final appearance of the woven material, that is, the way in which the threads are crossed. The strands called 'warp' threads are set up vertically and parallel to each other, then the strands referred to as 'weft' threads are woven horizontally across them. The warp and weft threads therefore cross at right angles to each other, although there are exceptions to this in hand weaving.

The pattern produced by the warp and weft threads shows how the fabric has been woven, with vertical gaps for the position of the warp, and horizontal rows for the position of the weft. In theory, this represents a

technical diagram from which a weaver could work. In the diagrams below, the raised warp thread is shown by the black squares, while the empty squares indicate that the weft thread is visible, as the warp thread has been taken under it. From these patterns, the design of the weave becomes apparent and would be enough to tell you about the weave of the whole piece of fabric.

There are three main types of weaving, on which all others are based; plain weave, twill weave and sateen weave. A brief explanation of each is given in the table below, together with an indication of the type of silk you should purchase.

Type of weave	Design and pattern of the weave	Fabrics
Plain weave is the simplest and has the smallest possible pattern. The weave is smooth and looks the same from both sides. Cotton weavers call this 'cotton weave', wool weavers 'cloth weave' and silk weavers 'taffeta weave'.		Chiffon, Georgette, Crêpe de Chine, Soleil, Habutai, Pongé, Toile, Organzine, Dupion, Tussore, Honan, Shantung, Taffeta, Spun silk, Noil silk.
In twill weave, each weft thread goes over several warp threads before being woven underneath. Lines can be seen on the surface of the weave, either in an S-shape or a Z-shape, according to their direction. Whether you choose a warp twill or a weft twill will depend on the thread you wish to predominate on the right side of the fabric.		S-shape Z-shape Twill
In sateen weave the cross-over points are not regular but are scattered all over the weave. This weave is comparatively light and soft. The weft threads are pushed up close to each other and create a smooth and glossy effect.		Satin and Satin crêpe. Weft threads over-twisted, warp threads twisted normally.

Testing colours on silk

This page illustrates how colour can affect each fabric in a different way. Only a drop of colour was allowed to drip on to each one but, as you can see, the colour spreads out according to the thickness of the material and the composition of the weave.

On fine fabrics a drop of colour spreads across a much larger area than on thick and coarse materials. This is important to the silk painter, because it means that the thickness of the silk must be taken into account when calculating how much colour to use. For this reason, it is better to prepare too much paint than too little, especially when painting large areas as it is difficult to duplicate the exact tone.

The differences in the application of gutta, see page 52, and the varied effects that can be created with salt, see page 48, should also be borne in mind.

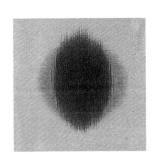

Silk satin

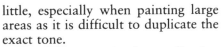

Habutai

Pongé

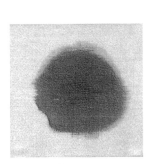

Taffeta

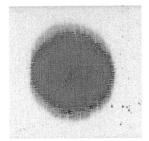

Chiffon

Crêpe georgette

Crêpe de Chine

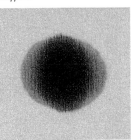

Satin crêpe

Twill

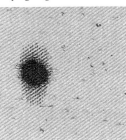

Twill

Toile

Indian dupion

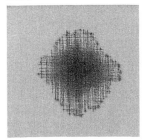

Tussore

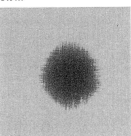

Honan

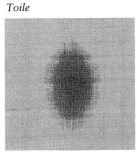

Honan

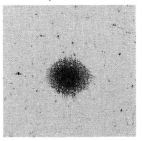

Noil

A review of silk materials

	Trade name Weight in gm	Material/weave/characteristics	Suggestions for use
SYNTHETIC SILK	**Chiffon** 20gm	Originally a French nickname for the working-classes: fine thread, transparent, veil-type crêpe in a taffeta weave.	Evening dresses, scarves, shawls.
	Crêpe georgette 21gm	Soft, crêpe-like taffeta weave; strongly over-twisted warp and weft threads; somewhat thicker and heavier than chiffon.	Evening dresses, blouses, scarves.
	Crêpe de Chine 50–75gm	Literally, Chinese crêpe; not very highly twisted, fine warp threads; over-twisted, coarse weft threads; taffeta weave; crease-resistant weave, grainy appearance.	Dresses, blouses, scarves, shawls.
	Satin crêpe 53–55gm	Crêpe-like sateen weave with very thick normally twisted warp and over-twisted weft threads; right side smooth and glossy, underside matt and rough; falls softly.	Dresses, blouses, lingerie.
	Silk satin 50–53gm	Satin is actually a group name for sateen weaves. Satin weave is made from normally twisted threads; particularly noticeable is the smooth, very glossy surface.	Party dresses, jackets, scarves, cushions, pictures, lingerie.
	Habutai	Fine taffeta weave from Japan, also called Japanese silk.	Dresses, scarves.
	Pongé 05 20–22gm 06 24–26gm 08 32–34gm 010 42–44gm 012 50–52gm 014 66–68gm	Smooth, light silk; taffeta weave without additional weighting; comes in a variety of weights.	Dresses, scarves, shawls; because the colours flow so well, it is the favourite material for silk painting.
	Taffeta 52–60gm	Particularly thick and slightly stiff taffeta weave; warp threads finer than weft threads; finely fluted, smooth surface.	Lining material. umbrella material; occasionally used for cocktail or evening dresses.
	Twill 42–45gm	Thick, supple, glossy twill weave; distinguished by its lines of diagonal fluting, or twill lines.	Dresses, shawls, ties, scarves, lining material, cushions, jackets.
	Toile	Fine threads; soft, flowing taffeta weave.	Dresses, blouses, shirts.
	Plissée	Fine material; permanently pressed and pleated into narrow folds.	Dresses, skirts.
	Organzine 26gm	Soft chiffon-like taffeta weave; partly made from the finest silk which has not had the bast removed; naturally stiffened.	Blouses, dresses, home textiles.
WILD SILK	**Dupion** 80–110gm	Delightful 'knop' fabric made from flawed, blemished or double cocoons; the term 'dupion' means two caterpillars that have spun cocoons together; warp of mulberry silk, weft of rough tussore or spun thread.	Dresses, jackets.
	Tussore silk	Silk from the tussore, or oak moth; rustic appearance from thickened and knopped warp and weft threads.	Dresses, blouses, trousers, coats, jackets, skirts, home textiles, lampshades.
	Honan silk	Named after the Chinese province of Honan; tussore silk in taffeta weave with knopped thickening of warp and weft threads; strong but with finer threads than Shantung.	As for tussore silk.
	Shantung	Named after the Chinese province of Shantung; coarse, taffeta weave of tussore silk.	As for tussore silk.
MIXED WEAVES	**Spun silk**	Warp and weft of spun silk in taffeta weave; a mixture of the more coarse types has a warp of spun silk and weft of noil silk.	Dresses, blouses, shirts, home textiles.

Jacquard silk

This patterned fabric was named after the Frenchman, Joseph Marie Jacquard, (1752–1834), who invented the Jacquard machine in 1805 while working at his home as a silk weaver. This device was fitted to a loom and was operated by punchcards. It automatically raised and lowered the warp threads, to produce a figured fabric. Today, almost any pattern, small or large, can be produced by machine; for example, large figured damask fabrics, richly embellished brocades and knitted textiles with artistic scenes.

When Jacquard silk fabrics are dyed, they take on a pattern of light and shade, either light against a dark background or vice versa. As the fabric moves, it shimmers where light hits the surface. A reverse effect is produced by the complementary pattern on the other side of the fabric.

Figured fabrics, with a self-pattern, can be painted in the same way as crêpe or silk satin but gutta and salt techniques are not really effective. The samples given here show the front and reverse sides of three Jacquard fabrics.

Jacquard silk with a square pattern, front and reverse sides.

Jacquard silk with a lively textured surface pattern, front and reverse sides.

Jacquard silk with a wavy, diamond-shaped pattern, front and reverse sides.

Hints on buying and caring for silk

Silk is a sensitive natural material, so it is important to take note of the following hints. Just as you should give your skin special attention to keep it soft and supple, so silk should be treated with the same gentle care. Harsh washing methods and intense sunlight should always be avoided.

If you are considering having a silk garment cleaned professionally, be warned that not all cleaning companies will accept a hand-painted item, let alone give any guarantee for its treatment. Garments which have gold and silver gutta outlines should never be dry cleaned.

Which silk for which purpose?

When it comes to choosing which silk fabric to buy, almost any pure silk material can be used for silk painting, but some are more difficult to handle than others. Fine pongé silks, numbers 5, 6 and 8, are particularly recommended for beginners, as their smooth surface absorbs the paint easily. They are also fairly inexpensive, so a novice who wishes to experiment will not be too worried about mistakes! Wild silk, by comparison, is rather unmanageable as the gutta and paints do not penetrate the surface.

Ideas for using the different types of silk are given in the last column of the chart on page 28.

Should silk be washed beforehand?

Before you begin to paint on silk, there are a few points to consider. If the material contains any impregnation or finishing agent, the paints tend to run off the surface, so these fabrics should be washed before use. Silk purchased from a specialist shop is normally untreated, so you can save yourself work and time.

Another important point to consider is that of shrinkage, and having spent time and effort on making a silk garment, it might all be wasted after the first wash. It is difficult to predict how much shrinkage will occur, as it varies for each type of silk, but it could be as much as 10% of the length. It is much easier to immerse the material in hand-hot water beforehand, then stretch it out to dry on a frame before painting. When the paint is dry, you can cut out the pattern without having to worry about making any alterations.

Some garments also include knitted sections. You must then bear in mind that pure silk knitting is not as elastic, and does not retain its shape as well as wool, with its naturally springy fibres. Over a period of time, silk knitting may stretch by up to 10%. It is worth making up a sample of the knitting, about 15cm (6in) square, then wash it and hang it up to dry, before casting on the exact number of stitches. If you wash the skeins of silk and hang them up to dry before beginning to knit, you will also avoid the problem of stretching.

How should silk be washed?

1) Handwashing in lukewarm water, up to 40°C (105°F), using a special powder for fine fabrics, is recommended. Do not use shampoo, because it contains conditioning ingredients that may damage the silk. After washing, rinse thoroughly in warm water. To brighten the colours, add a little white vinegar to the final rinse.
2) Thin fabrics should be gently squeezed out, rolled up briefly in a thick, absorbent cotton towel, and squeezed out again, but *not* wrung! Iron immediately with the iron on a wool setting.
3) Thick fabrics should be treated as fine fabrics, but after they have been squeezed out, it is better to hang them up in an absorbent towel so that they begin to dry before ironing. However, you must ensure that sections of the fabric do not touch each other because surplus colour could run off and cause stains. Put garments on an inflatable coat-hanger or place hand-towels between the pieces and in the sleeves. Finally, iron the fabric.
4) Freshly painted and treated fabrics should be left for a couple of days before washing. Some paint instructions state that if you do this, the colours will show up more vividly.
5) To remove any surplus colour that has not been absorbed by the fabric, soak the silk in cold water for a little while. This will not affect the brilliance of the colours.
6) To be on the safe side, hand-painted or printed silk fabrics should always be washed separately from other items, as they may not be completely colourfast.
7) For knitted silk, always lift the item out of the water very carefully, so that the weight of water does not stretch it. Lay it on a thick, absorbent towel to dry, patting it gently into shape.

How should silk be ironed?

1) Iron silk while it is still fairly wet. Use the wool setting on your iron.
2) Make sure that you don't press any seams, or they will go shiny!
3) Creases caused as you iron are best removed by wetting the fabric again, then ironing them out.
4) Afer ironing, leave silk to cool.

Painting on silk

Painting materials and equipment

The photograph shows a wide selection of various items which are available to the silk painters, but you should only choose those you need for your requirements. The basics you require are as follows:-

- Silk, cut to size with allowances.
- Wooden slate frame, on which to stretch the silk when painting.
- Adhesive tape to cover the frame, which can be renewed to prevent paint from one project marking another.
- Pins to fix the silk to the frame.
- Specialist silk painting colours.
- Distilled water and alcohol (methylated spirits) to thin the paint.
- Two water containers.
- Small, watertight containers, glass, for preparation, mixing, and storage of paints.
- Measuring jug for preparing the thinning mixture.
- Small syringes or droppers for precise colour mixing.
- Thin, and very thick painting brushes, plus cottonwool swabs, to apply paint.
- Gutta, or suitable preparation, water soluble, to provide outlines.
- Metal-tipped applicator bottle to apply the gutta.
- Gutta solvent (benzine or lighter fuel), for thinning the colourless gutta, or for storing nib attachments.
- Salt crystals in a variety of grain sizes.
- Hairdryer.

- Suitable means of fixing the paints, depending on the type of paint; ironing, steam-setting, fixing agent.
- Absorbent cottonwool or kitchen towels.
- Scissors.
- Newspaper, or waste paper, to prevent staining, and for steam-fixing.

Silk paints

Painting on silk is still frequently confused with batik, which originated in Java. In both techniques, areas of fabric are blocked out and then the remainder is coloured. In batik, however, patterns are drawn on the fabrics with wax and then the fabric is immersed in dye. This wax is removed and a further layer applied to different areas, and the fabric is dipped in another colour. This process can be repeated as many times as required.

A similar resist technique is used in silk painting, the pattern outlines being drawn with gutta, which stops the colours spreading out, see page 52. Liquid paints are then used to paint within the outlines, either mixed separately beforehand, or applied directly on to the silk. The paints can be dissolved in water, or a mixture of water and alcolhol, and even when the paint has been allowed to dry, you can lighten the colours if you wish.

The old tradition of silk painting has been given a modern approach in terms of quality and brilliance of paints, but the basic technique of painting remains the same. Nowadays we expect to have durable colours that do not fade, or run when washed, and this could not be achieved by the old methods. Also, the traditional way of preparing the silk with a starch mixture, to prevent the colours flowing into each other, is no longer satisfactory, as the fabric must be washable and drape softly, especially when used for garments that are worn frequently. In place of the water colours and Indian ink that were used in ancient days, the chemical industry has developed a range of colours and substances to meet our modern requirements. There are also various ways of influencing, or completely controlling the flow of the colours, see pages 60–61.

You can now purchase a whole range of specialist paints suitable for use on silk and wool (animal natural fibres), on cotton and linen (plant natural fibres), and also on artificial mixed fibres. However, apart from one product which has just recently come on to the market, *none* of them are guaranteed not to fade or for colour-fastness when washed, but these two requirements are essential for all textiles. To make a paint colour durable and resistant to fading, therefore, the material has to undergo a fixing process after the painting is completed during which the paint becomes 'set' into the weave.

There are three different methods of fixing; iron-setting paints, those that are set with chemical products and those that require steam-setting. Before making your choice you should consider the differences between them and weigh up the pros and cons, because the final results and the cost of the fixing process can vary quite a lot. To help you decide, more details of the three methods are given on page 34 but in order to fully illustrate steam-fixing, which may appear to be rather complicated, the different steps in the process are explained on page 62. Prior to fixing, the painted fabric is extremely fragile and must be handled carefully. It is sensitive to water, alcohol and light.

Efficient methods of breeding silk worms and progress in the chemical industry have now brought silk fabrics and painting materials well within the reach of all who are interested in this art form.

Hints on storing paints

- Liquid paints are best stored in the dark, where it is not too cold or warm.
- Keep the manufacturer's colour concentrated pigments and your thinned, or mixed, working colours separated in watertight containers.
- Paint containers made from clear glass, or transparent plastic are best; a light shake makes the paint run up the sides of the container to give a reliable indication of the tone, as the layer of colour is very thin and lets the light shine through – just as with painted silk!

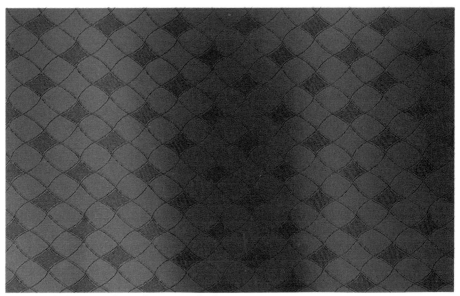

Jacquard silk painted in soft stripes of colour.

Iron-setting paints

Many different brands are now available from craft shops but you *must always* follow the instructions given by the manufacturer of the product you choose. As a general guide, all you need to do to fix these colours is to iron the dry painted silk on the reverse side with an iron set on heat level 2, for two of three minutes.

Depending on the make of paint, the painted item can sometimes be immersed in cold water, to which a drop of white vinegar has been added, before it is ironed. When you do this most of the gutta resist comes off and any colour that has overflowed is also removed. Dry the silk by laying it flat on an absorbent towel, and roll it up to remove excess moisture. While still in this damp state it can then be ironed dry, with the iron set on 'wool'. If the silk sticks to the iron at this stage it means that not all of the resist has been removed. It must be washed again and your iron cleaned. Only when it is ironed does the colour develop its full brilliance. Once it is fixed, the silk can be washed at temperatures of up to 30°C (86°F).

The advantage of paints set by ironing is that you do not need any equipment, other than that usually found in any household. As it is easy enough for a child to do, it is suitable for school projects. With this method the reaction of salt is very good but the flowing effect achieved with this technique is sometimes slowed down. Water and alcohol techniques, however, are not so satisfactory as the silk, which is stiffened by the painting, becomes soft again when washed.

Tests carried out recently have shown that iron-setting paints are also steam-fixable. With this process, they acquire a more brilliant colour than is possible with iron-setting.

Chemically-fixed paints

For some ranges of paint, the manufacturers also provide fixing agents under various trade names, to cope with the problem of setting the paint. When these are applied to the painted and dried piece of silk, while still stretched in the frame, the colours are fixed by a chemical reaction with the fabric.

The fixing agent must be spread very rapidly over the front of the painted fabric, and on both the front and the back of thick materials. After a reaction time of 60–90 minutes, the fixing process is complete and the silk can be rinsed in cold water. Tests with this method, however, have shown that when the fixing agent is applied to the silk, particles of paint may be removed which could possibly be transferred to other areas and cause stains. Also, the colours are not as brilliant as steam-set paints and rinsing out the fixing agent can be rather involved.

Steam-setting paints

If you steam-fix your paints, the colours are up to four times brighter than with other methods. Many different brands are available and if you ask a professional silk painter for their choice of paint, they will almost certainly mention one of these products.

With this fixing process, the silk and colours are bound permanently together with hot steam. If you have a pressure cooker, you can easily do this in your own home. Special steam ovens are available for this purpose, but it is only worth the expense if you use this item on a regular basis, otherwise there will almost certainly be a craft shop near you which offers a similar fixing service. It is worth paying for this, as your painting will be fixed expertly and quickly. The pros and cons of the various steam-setting processes, and precise instructions for steam-fixing can be found on pages 62–63. More and more paints now come into this category and if you purchase a particular product which requires ironing or chemical fixing, you will probably find that the same manufacturer offers a range of steam-setting colours.

When deciding on which type of silk paint to purchase, you would be well advised to choose a steam-setting one, but the final choice will depend on the following points:-

- The brands which are available, and will remain available in your district.
- Which brands have been used for work you have seen and admired.
- Which brands are recommended in courses that your have attended, or would like to attend.
- The type of painting for which the brand is required and whether it is to be carried out by children or adults.

Hints on mixing different products

- According to the instructions for use, most manufacturers guarantee that the colours within their range of paints are completely mixable with each other, and can also be thinned down with water or alcohol to give the most delicate pastel tones. Tests have also proved that paints of different brands can be used with other fixing processes, although only steam-setting is really suitable for all of them.
- Before beginning to paint, you should be aware that not all brands of paint are equally suitable for all silk painting techniques. However, in view of the fact that you now have more freedom of choice in the fixing process, you are not necessarily confined to one brand. In spite of this, if you want to adapt techniques for your own individual design, you should carry out mixing, setting and washing tests on a small piece of silk before beginning a project.

Brushes

You should choose a brush that absorbs and holds a lot of colour, so that you can complete large areas without having to lift the brush away from the fabric to dip it in the paint again. The most versatile brush is one with a very broad head and bristles that spread out in front, so that smaller areas can also be filled in carefully. The thickness of the bristles must be determined by the thickness of the fabric and the amount of paint which has to be absorbed, also on the subject to be painted.

Brushes with artificial bristles can be used for silk painting but Chinese, or Japanese, bamboo brushes are better. The bristles are made from bamboo fibres and because the central bristles are short and the outer ones long, they can absorb an astonishing amount of paint, without dripping when in use. The bristles look tousled in their dry state but, handled carefully, they form into a fine point as soon as they come into contact with liquid. They are suitable for both bold and delicate patterns, so you don't need a huge collection of brushes.

A ball of cottonwool, rolled up and held with a clothes peg, is a good way of applying colour quickly to a large area. If you use it on small areas, however, it is rather fiddly and tends to leave wisps behind. You can experiment with rolled up strips of cloth but these are sometimes too stiff and release the paint too slowly. Small sponges also drip too easily and too much paint is lost.

Small paint containers with brush attachments can also be obtained but these have to be used with great precision, so that too much colour is not released at once. They are rather awkward to clean and it is best to use them for colouring large areas only,

to avoid refilling with another colour. If you wrap them in aluminium foil to stop them drying out, they can be left filled up for a couple of days.

The method you use for applying paint is a matter of personal choice and the design you have in mind but a good quality brush has many advantages. If you have filled it with too much paint, it can be wiped off on the edge of the container, so that most of the unused colour is not wasted. It is also more comfortable to handle and can stand up to more vigorous use.

Working area

If it is possible, try to ensure that you have an area where you can leave work which you have started but not completed. Very often the best ideas come to you after you have taken a break from painting for a couple of hours.

Good lighting is also essential and the best place is near a window, as you need daylight for mixing the colours, so that you can see the subtleties of tone. Fluorescent lighting is satisfactory but remember that yellow artificial light changes the appearance of colours.

Your work table should be large enough to allow a frame 90 × 90cm

(36 × 36in) to be placed on it without wobbling, and with some room on either side for your brushes and paints. The surface should be washable, or protected by several layers of newspaper. As an alternative, trestles can be used at either end as rests for a large frame. The frame should be secured to the trestles, so that it doesn't accidently slip off as you are painting. You will also need a separate area for your other painting equipment, standing next to the frame.

A comfortable seat is essential and, if possible, one where the height can be adjusted to allow you to reach all areas of the fabric. A piano stool or office chair is ideal.

As paint containers can sometimes be knocked over, it is a good idea to protect a carpet with sheets of newspaper around your work area. You may also need to wrap an apron around yourself!

Hints on caring for brushes
- Clean your brushes after use with soap and rinse them well with plenty of clean water.
- Smooth the bristles back into shape after cleaning.
- Leave the brushes in a glass to dry, with the bristles pointing upwards.

Paint container with brush attachment and brushes in various sizes for backgrounds and filling in small areas.

Stretching the silk

Before you cut the silk to size, or begin painting it, make sure it does not contain any dressing, or is likely to shrink, see page 30.

The silk must be stretched taut and be fully supported while it is being painted, so a frame is essential. An old wooden picture frame, an artist's stretcher, laths of wood glued together, a batik frame, or an adjustable slate frame can all be used for this purpose. The choice of frame will obviously depend on the size of the painting, and if you plan to tackle projects of different sizes, then it will be more practical to use a frame with adjustable attachments.

fig 1   fig 2   fig 3

To prevent paints penetrating into the wood, plastic masking tape should be stuck along the edges of the frame. This would not be necessary for your first project, but as you continue with other designs, contact with the damp silk could cause old colours left on the frame to stain the fabric. It is important to wipe the masking tape clean with a damp cloth before new silk is stretched out, and to renew it completely from time to time. Paper masking tape is not really suitable for this purpose, because it also absorbs colour and then deposits it again, so it must be renewed for each piece of work.

The wood used for the frame must be soft enough to allow drawing pins, or three-pronged pins, to be pushed into it to secure the silk in place. It must also be strong enough not to twist or bend when the silk is stretched taut. Ordinary drawing pins, see Figure 1, or notice-board pins, see Figure 2, can be used but three-pronged pins, see Figure 3, are the best ones for the job and should be part of a silk painter's equipment. These allow the tension to be spread over three points and therefore lessen the possibility of tearing fine silk.

When you stretch the silk in the frame, first fasten the four corners, then secure it along each parallel side. The pins should not be placed directly opposite each other, see Figure 4, but slightly staggered, see Figure 5. This will prevent stretch lines, or tight raised sections in the silk that will interfere with the painting by allowing colour to collect in puddles between them. However, you must ensure that the material is not being stretched at an angle which, especially after using an outlining agent such as gutta, can cause difficulties in the fixing. The silk will change shape when it is removed from the frame

Stretching out silk for painting.

but the outlining agent will not and this will create 'waves' in the fabric. If you trace the lines of the warp and weft threads in the silk, you can clearly see which sections have relaxed and which have tightened. The closer together you place the pins, the less likelihood there is of any distortion in the silk. A gap of between 5−8cm (2−3¼ in) is ideal.

Because of the position of these pins, it is not possible to paint across the entire width of a piece of silk. For one thing, the holes left by the pins will allow colour to seep through the silk, and stains can also be caused by the actual contact of the silk with the wooden frame, where it has not been masked. So in order to have a piece of silk on which colour is evenly applied all over, provision must be made for an allowance of silk which can be torn off when the work is finished. There are exceptions to this, such as a design which is to be used as a picture, where the edges will eventually be hidden by a frame.

Another unwanted effect may be created during painting if the silk is allowed to sag in the middle of the frame, and touch the surface of the table on which the frame is placed. This causes the colours to spread too rapidly in the loosened weave of the fabric and drops of colour will collect together at the lowest point. One solution to this problem is to increase the distance between the silk and the work surface by placing small wooden blocks beneath each corner of the frame, but you must secure them to avoid the frame slipping.

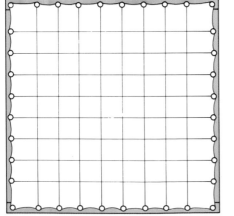

fig 4: incorrect way to stretch silk

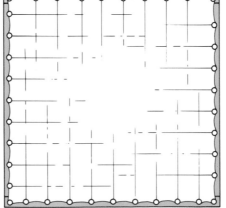

fig 5: pins are staggered

Long screws may also be used in each corner to give the frame additional height but the ends must be protected by corks, to prevent them scratching the work surface. If the material continues to sag, it is essential to remove the pins, stretch the fabric and secure it again.

The best answer to the problem is to use a batik frame, as this can be adjusted in steps of 5cm (2in). This is particularly useful when the silk begins to stretch with the wetness from the paint, as the sides can be tightened with butterfly wing nuts to achieve the correct tension again. An adjustable slate frame, used for embroidery and quilting is also satisfactory.

The size of the frame you require is determined by your choice of fabric and design, as the width of the material will already be pre-set. If you want to paint a longer length of material, it can be fixed vertically to two frames, positioned one above the other. You may find it difficult to stretch the silk evenly, however, because it will only be attached horizontally to the side edges of both frames, and the lower edge of one frame and the top edge of the other.

Do-it-yourself painting frame

If you don't want to buy a frame immediately, or you just want to try out silk painting for the first time, you can quite easily make your own inexpensive frame by following these instructions. The size is based on the most popular width for silk fabric, 92cm (36in), as exactly half of this size can be stretched out, so there is no unnecessary trimming needed. The size is just right for one side of a cusion 40cm (16in) square.

With a small frame it is easier to glue the corners, rather than use screws, also, the heads of the screws may get in the way of the pins when you are securing the silk. Larger frames for items such as scarves become unwieldy and for this purpose a frame that is slotted or bolted together is more practical, see pages 38–39. This can also be stored away when not in use without taking up too much space.

The frame suggested here should be made from timber that is at least 4cm (1½ in) high. Additional blocks are then unnecessary, as when the silk is wet and sags in the middle it will not come into contact with the table.

Materials

- 4 planed lengths of wood that is not too hard, cross-section 2 × 4cm (¾ × 1½ in), 46cm (18in) long.
- Small saw.
- Ruler.
- Pencil.
- Set square.
- Wood glue.
- 4 clamps.

Instructions

- On both ends of each length of wood mark the sections to be cut out, using the set square and pencil, see diagram below.
- Cut out the corners with the saw, leaving the pencil marks visible in order to achieve an exact fit.
- Lay the strips of wood out in a square; two strips with sawn out ends pointing upwards, the other two with ends pointing downwards, see diagram.
- Place some glue on the sawn ends.
- Hold the corners together with clamps, see diagram, until the glue has set. Remove any surplus glue and leave to harden.

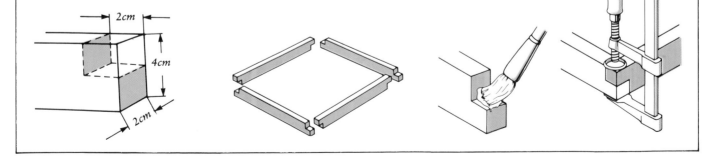

Comparison of different types of frames

Number	1	2	3
Type of frame	Glued frame	Slotted frame	Frame with bolts
Construction	Four side pieces with corners stuck on top of one another	Four side pieces with slots sawn out every 5cm (2in)	Side pieces joined by wing nuts through holes at 5cm (2in) intervals, with protective caps for raising the frame
Top view			
Side view			
Stretching the silk	Flush surface	Flush surface	Raised surface
Advantages	• Good value and simple to make yourself • Silk on one level	• Relatively good value • Adjustable size	• Simple to make yourself • Not restricted to right angles
Disadvantages	• Cannot be dismantled • Fixed in one size	• Only adjustable in fixed slots	• Only adjustable in fixed slots • Silk not stretched on one level
		With all adjustable frames there is one great disadvantage if you want to paint a small area on a very large frame, say about 100cm (40in): the ends of the side pieces will stick out and get in your way as you paint. It is well worth buying a frame which has a combination of long and short side pieces.	

4	5	6	7
Frame with sliding bolts	Frame with wing bolts	Sliding frame	Sliding frame
Side pieces joined with wing nuts bolted through slots, with protective caps for raising the frame	Side pieces joined by wing nuts bolted through slots in the side; the frame is altered by tightening or loosening the wing nuts	Four side pieces which join together through metal corner joints and are fixed with pins	Four side pieces which join together through metal guides and are fixed with pins screwed into each end
Raised surface	Flush surface	Flush surface	Flush surface
• Silk can be stretched again • Not restricted to right angles	• Silk can be stretched again • Silk on one level	• Silk can be stretched again • Silk on one level	• Silk can be stretched again • Silk on one level
• Silk not stretched on one level			

Frames 5–7 have side pieces that stick out on all four sides when on a small setting, so you virtually need to quadruple your working area. In fact, the smaller you set your frame the more space it takes up because of the protruding side pieces.
Frames 3 and 4 can be fitted with extra long screws with protective caps, which act as a stand to raise the frame. In this way you can avoid large pieces of fabric sagging on to the table when wet.

Preparing the paints

Silk painting colours are sold as liquid concentrates. If they are used in their pure form they tend to saturate most types of silk and during washing, even after the fixing process, surplus colour bleeds out. To counteract this the colour concentrate should be thinned, or blended, before use.

Ascertain whether the paints you buy are meant to be thinned with water alone, or with both water and alcohol. Prepare your working colours by putting a few drops of the concentrated paint for each tone into a separate watertight beaker, then blend them with the correct thinning agent. Take note that water and alcohol not only thin the paint but also have a distinct effect on the painting technique.

Alcohol

Either pure alcohol from the chemist or methylated spirits encourage the paint to penetrate the fabric and helps it to spread evenly. However, it is not suitable to use on its own as a thinning agent, as it evaporates too quickly. This causes the paint to dry too quickly and can result in hard edges where the paints meet.

Water

Used on its own as a thinner, water has a tendency to keep the silk damp for some time, which is something you may not always want. It helps the paint to penetrate the fabric and spread evenly, but to a lesser extent than alcohol. If you live in an area noted for very hard or soft water, you can overcome the problem by using distilled water.

Alcohol and water

By experimenting with a blend of alcohol and water you can influence the behaviour of the paint to achieve the effect you require. The best proportions to use for thinning paint concentrate with alcohol and water is one part alcohol to three parts water, (preferably distilled). With this mixture the colours are absorbed more evenly and they also dry fairly quickly.

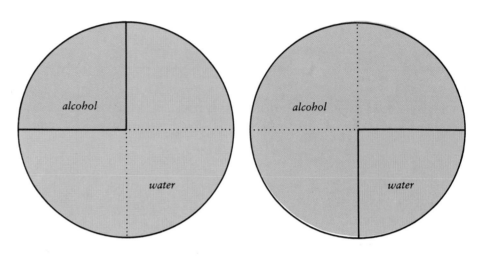

Best proportions for thinning paints.   *Alcohol-water mixture for pastel shades.*

A mixture of this ratio will improve the flow of the paint, even when painting on wild silk. This fabric can sometimes be unmanageable because of its structure and the paint only seeps very slowly into the weave.

For normal use one part of paint concentrate should be added to the same amount of thinning mixture and this will only lessen the intensity of the colour very slightly. Black is the only exception to this, and it should always be thinned by the minimum amount recommended by the paint manufacturer.

Depending on what additional effects are required, you can alter the proportion of water to alcohol in the thinning agent and also the ratio of paint to thinner. To thin the paints to give very soft pastel colours, the proportion of alcohol can be raised until the ratio is reversed to three parts alcohol to one part water. More information is given in the respective section in the following chapter.

Hints for diluting paints

— It is more convenient to calculate the amounts of thinning liquid in litres (pints), ie, fill a bottle which holds 1 litre (1¾ pints) with 250ml (9 fluid oz) alcohol and 750ml (25 fluid oz) distilled water. This ensures accurate proportions. The bottle should always be well shaken before use, because after a short time the alcohol rises to the top of the water.

— Similarly, 1 litre (1¾ pints) of paint concentrate mixed with the same amount of thinning agent can be kept indefinitely in a watertight container, away from heat. The alcohol in the mixture will separate, so it should be shaken before use.

— For larger areas, especially of thick absorbent fabrics, it is always better to mix too much colour than too little, as it is virtually impossible to repeat exactly the same tone at a later stage.

Silk painting effects

You can achieve a whole range of spectacular effects with silk painting, which give it a special appeal and distinguish it from other creative art forms. The actual painting process itself is of great importance, not merely a particular design or technique. Unexpected results can be discovered by trying out different methods, in fact, studying the paint and its behaviour are what make silk painting so exciting. This chapter will introduce you to a few tricks of the trade and encourage you to experiment for yourself.

Paint characteristics

Many of the techniques described here would not be possible at all if the paints used for silk painting did not display special characteristics. These unique properties form the basis of all the examples described.

Unlike conventional paints, which are opaque and basically lie on the surface of the material, silk painting colours penetrate the fabric completely and, depending on the thickness of the material, create colouring of almost the same intensity on both the front and reverse sides. Light is able to shine through both the silk and the paint to create a brilliant, transparent effect.

To enable all the paint to soak into the fabric, the silk should not have been treated or dressed beforehand. To check this, put a drop of colour on one edge; if it rolls off then you will have to wash the silk before you stretch it out, see page 30. If the colour sinks into the silk, then you can go ahead with the painting. In fact, most types of silk sold specifically for silk painting can be used without washing them beforehand.

The type of weave also affects the absorption of the paint and this is shown very clearly on page 27. The

△ *Red tree showing effect achieved with salt.*

Detail showing colour separation. ▷

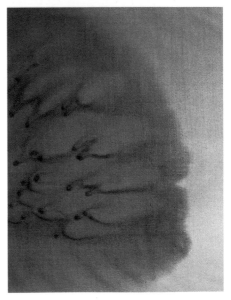

way in which the paint flows is also determined by whether the silk is to be painted wet or dry, the way it is stretched and whether overall anti-fusant preparations, or outlining methods have been applied.

The examples on the opposite page show quite clearly the difference in colour absorption between dry and wet silk. You will also see that if mixed colours are used, their components spread out in the silk at different speeds. In the right-hand example the blue has merged into the other colours. This is because the water in the silk has slowed down the drying time of the paint, and the blue has had sufficient time to spread out.

The detail from the picture of the red tree on the previous page also shows that similar separations of colour can occur with the salt technique. Using this method will create more intense tones of colour in the painting than you would have thought possible from the limited palette you are using.

The direction in which paints prefer to spread out is shown in the following experiments. If you dab colour very carefully on to pongé silk with a fine brush, you don't get a spot – you will have a small cross! In most instances, even a drop of water will not spread into a round circle but is seen as a blob which seems to follow the weave. The paint normally spreads along warp threads more quickly than weft threads, running from one selvedge to the other, especially if the silk is more tightly stretched in this direction. However, this is only true of smooth silks, as silks, with thicker or slubbed weft threads will have a different effect on the direction of the paint.

The other example shows how you can limit the way the paint runs by placing spots of similar size really quickly next to each other, as they all obstruct each other and form common borders. You can also use water, alcohol and salt to create this effect.

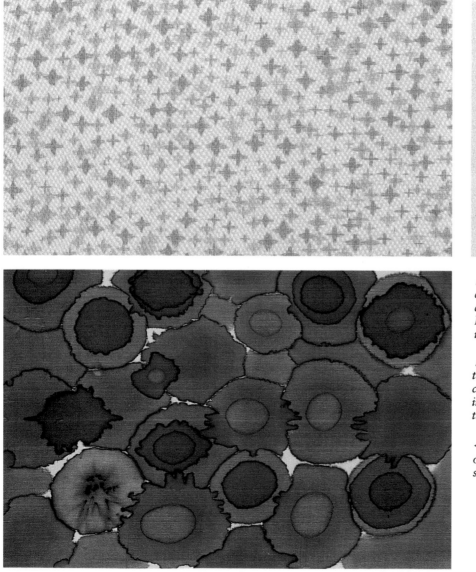

△ The two columns above show the difference in colour absorption between dry (left-hand) and wet (right-hand) silk. Exactly the same amount of colour was used each time.

△ If you dab tiny drops of colour on to the silk, you can clearly see from the cross-shapes that are created the direction in which the paint prefers to spread; along the warp and weft of the weave.

◁ Placing spots of colour next to each other quickly shows how they form shared borders.

Colour tones separated by gutta.

Even without gutta, there are borders.

Achieving layering of colours.

Colour blending

One of the most important creative effects in silk painting is to achieve well-blended layerings of colour, instead of painting all the areas in colours of just one tone. In nature you will never find colours without subtle nuances and even a cloudless sky has a spread of tones of blue from one horizon to the other. The variety of shades become even richer in the morning and evening hours. By using 'washing' techniques, you can easily achieve such effects yourself.

To obtain a soft blend between two colours, mix at least two intermediate tones beforehand. The number of tones and the amount of colour will obviously depend on the size of the piece of silk. On silk that has previously been dampened with water, lay the colours next to each other and gently rub the silk under more water until you achieve the shading you require. If you want stronger colours, then you must increase the density of the paint by not thinning it too much. Alternatively, you can apply more colour when the first application has been allowed to dry. Any irregularities which appear on the surface are evened out of their own accord by the slow drying process, especially if you are working on heavier silks.

The examples at the top of this page show that two in-between tones have been mixed with the first colour, yellow, and the last colour, blue. In the first column they have been painted next to each other but are separated by lines of gutta. In the centre, the colours have been painted next to each other without using gutta and they have begun to merge but there is still some natural separation. The last example shows the successful merger; the colours were painted next to each other on dampened silk and gently rubbed with a brush until a continuous blend was achieved.

Hints on colour blending

- Keep two glasses of clean water handy; one to clean the brushes and the other to use for brushing the colours into each other.
- The thicker the brush used for blending, the more even the results.
- It helps the paints to flow correctly if the silk is only stretched out on two opposite sides, so that the absorption of the colour has to follow the direction of the stretching.

43

Colour displacement

As explained on the previous page, one of the special properties of silk paints is that as long as they are wet, they can be transferred from one part of the silk to another. Even when they have dried, they can still be moved around to create different effects, prior to fixing, see page 34.

The landscape shown below is painted entirely in tones of blue without using any gutta, and yet it has distinct outlines that imitate the shape of a landscape. This effect has been created by colour displacement, and in order to achieve something similar, colour is first applied evenly to the silk. At the edges of the areas of colour you will obtain colour separation, see page 41, and in the detail on the same page a reddish patch is still visible on the left-hand side. This is because the blue contained in this colour runs at a different speed to the red and so the colour splits up into its original components of its own accord. While the paint was still wet, some salt was sprinkled on to the surface and because salt absorbs liquid, the pigments moved in the direction of the salt and light streaks were formed behind them. For further details of this technique, see page 48–51.

To spread the colours still further, after the paint had completely dried, water was dabbed next to the salt. It spread out in all directions and took pigments of colour with it. In the landscape example below, alcohol was placed on the dried paint. Here again, the light patch with a dark edge has been created, which does not, however, spread out as much as it did with water.

If you experiment you will be able to achieve partial loss and corresponding intensification of colour, without having to remove paint from the silk, or apply more. With salt, this effect is caused by absorption; with water and alcohol, by displacement, or washing out.

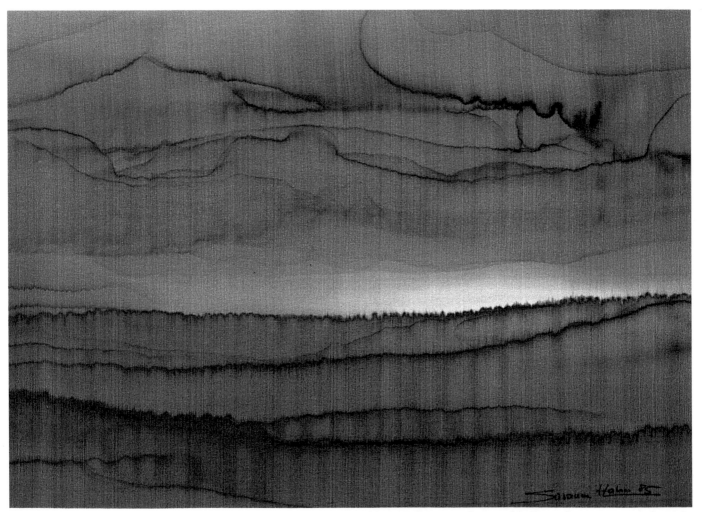

Landscape in tones of blue; the lines and contours have been created simply by colour displacement.

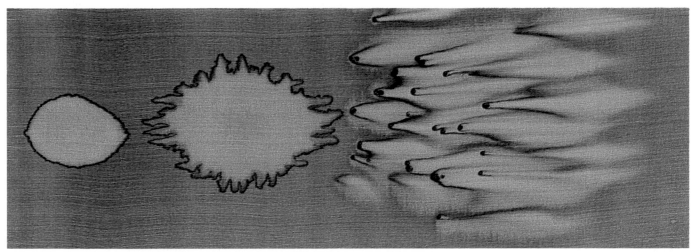

From right to left; salt has been placed on wet paint, water and alcohol on dry silk, using different colours for these three examples.

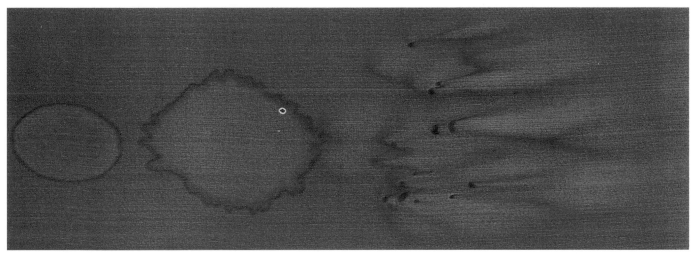

This example also shows the separation of the colours.

Here you can quite clearly see how the blue contained in the violet shade spreads outwards faster than the red.

Washing out technique

You must really explore the possibilities of this technique with your own experiments. The following tests are particularly recommended for those who are complete beginners at silk painting.

Apart from a frame, a piece of silk at least 45cm (17¾ in) square, suitable outlining preparation such as gutta, brush, water, alcohol and paint, all you will require is patience and a talent for observation. You should note down each individual step you take so that, later on, you will find it easier to appreciate how your results were developed.

Washing out experiment

Divide your stretched out piece of silk into six areas with the outlining preparation. The instructions give the order and sequence of the tests. It is best to carry out the four tests with different colours and, in particular, to repeat the alcohol tests several times. When you feel that you have mastered this principle, try it out on larger areas of fabric.

Wipe the whole area with water, without letting any puddles form. Drip paint on to the *wet* silk.	Colour the silk with normally thinned dark colour, then put spots or streaks of water on the still *wet* silk.
Colour the silk with normally thinned dark colour, then put spots or streaks of alcohol on the still *wet* colour.	Drip paint on to *dry* silk. Play around with this idea by placing different colours next to each other. Wait until the drops of paint have completely soaked into the fabric and dried, then overlay more layers of paint.
Colour the silk with normally thinned dark colour, then put spots or streaks of water on the colour when it has *dried*.	Colour the silk with normally thinned dark colour, then put spots or streaks of alcohol next to each other, when the colour has *dried*.

Results with wet silk	Results with dry silk
The most important point to note is that water and alcohol displace some of the colour and leave behind lighter areas. However, the spreading out of the colour, water and alcohol, is limited by the existing moisture in the material. Because of this, the amount of colour that soaks away is relatively slight. As the result of the less free-flowing colour mixture, spots and streaks of water and alcohol appear to be only slightly lightened, or partially tinted. Drops of alcohol applied to a damp area of paint cause a strong reaction at first, but this does become weaker as the slower-drying water gradually forces the basic colour out of the area and back to the patch of alcohol that has just dried. If you don't apply any more alcohol to the same spot, by the time the fabric has dried completely the colour will have spread out again, more or less evenly on the material.	In this sequence of tests, less resistance is shown to the drops of colour, water and alcohol, spreading out on the dry silk, so the spots are considerably larger than those applied to wet silk. Instead of the soft outlines of the 'wet on wet' technique described in the left-hand column, (watercolour technique), sharp, dark edges are formed where the colours collect together after they have spread out to the side. These edges are jagged to various degrees, according to the amount of liquid applied and the duration of the drying process; the longer it takes, the rougher the edge. Alcohol sinks more rapidly into the silk than water, and displaces previously applied paint more vigorously, so patches of alcohol normally appear lighter than patches of water. The relatively smooth edges are due to the fact that alcohol evaporates more quickly.

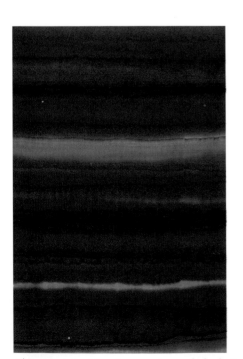

Experiment with colour, water and alcohol.

These examples of the washing out technique show the effects which can be achieved. In the example on page 46, the red surface area was lightened with yellow and similar colour tones. The parallel streaks were produced by alternate applications of colour, water and alcohol, which were allowed to dry each time. They were painted adjacent to and on top of one another.

In the grey pattern below, streaks of colour were applied first and when these horizontal bands had dried, water was applied in a slanting grid. The pattern on the right is similar to a folding, or binding dip-dyeing technique. You can find more examples on pages 89–92, giving suggestions for scarf patterns.

Variations you could explore might include, for example, a range of colour with light and dark contrasts; using complementary or contrasting colours, or colour on colour applications. Let your imagination run riot, to see what amazing results you can achieve!

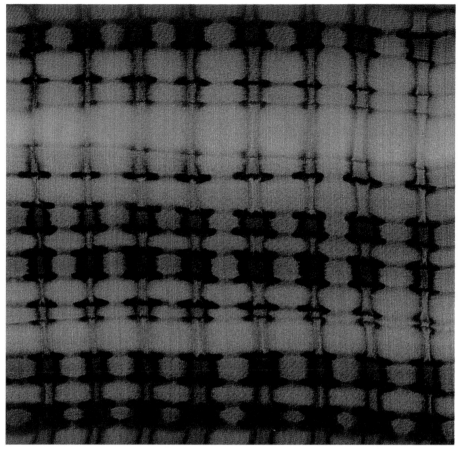

Experiment in washing out technique, using colour and water.

Here a grid of slanting lines has been applied with water and paint on a lightly striped background.

Salt technique

By sprinkling salt on to painted silk while it is still wet you can produce extremely attractive, if not completely controllable, effects. The ability of salt to absorb water, (a quality that is not quite so popular in the kitchen!), is used to advantage in this technique.

The moisture soaked up by the grains of salt has paint dissolved in it and this leaves traces behind on the fabric. According to the coarseness of the grains of salt, they form dark outlines, rings, streaks, or abstact shapes of varying delicacy. Some areas lose virtually all their colour, as the pigments collect together in a different place.

The effects produced by the salt will also depend on its condition. All salt absorbs moisture from the air while it is stored, so you should heat the salt before use in a saucepan or frying pan on the stove, in a microwave oven, or simply on a hot radiator, so that the moisture evaporates again and the salt becomes absorbent. It is worth keeping the salt you intend to use in a sealed container.

Salt has two effects on areas of colour; it can be used to lighten the colour, and it can break down mixed pigments into their basic components, see page 41. This depends largely on the flowing properties of the paint being used.

When using salt, the silk should not be too wet, or the grains of salt may dissolve completely, nor too dry, in which case it will produce only a very weak reaction, or none at all takes place. The salt continues to absorb the colour until it has completely dried out. If you need to move your piece of silk during this process, do ensure that the grains of salt do not roll around. They may come to rest in a different area and could spoil the effect you desire. The use of a hairdryer for special effects, or to accelerate the drying time, see page 58, is obviously not recommended with this technique.

As soon as the paint has dried, the salt should be carefully removed. Sweep the grains off the silk with a soft brush, otherwise they will eventually encrust the fabric. Grains of salt inadvertently left behind and fixed into the material will also cause stains, because of their excessive absorption of water from the steam, or fixing agent.

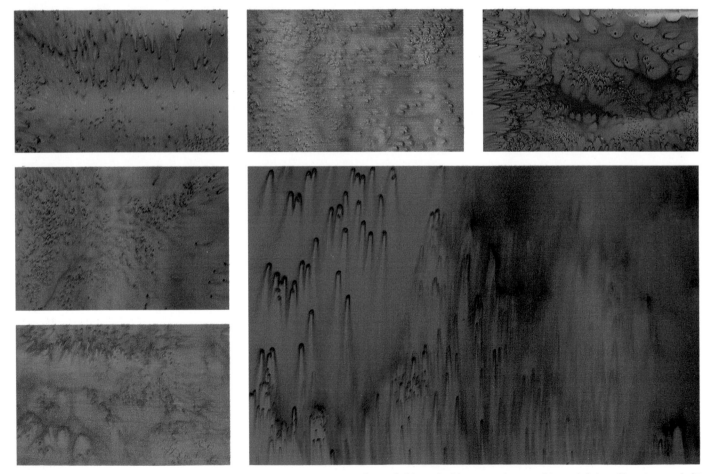

Salt effects on twill (top left), satin (top centre), pongé (top right), taffeta (centre left), chiffon (bottom left), and crêpe de Chine (bottom right).

Striking salt effects define the character of this landscape in blue.

Once an area has had salt sprinkled on it, it is very difficult to paint again, because tiny grains of salt adhere to the brush and interfere with the paint. If you place paint on a spot that has been lightened with salt, it will form an arc around it. There are certain advantages to be gained from this characteristic. You can, for example, reduce the spreading out of colour in the fabric by applying a base of salt solution beforehand, see page 60. You can also place grains of salt on an area and then brush paint directly on to them. With the latter technique you achieve typical hard edges, but remember to wash your brush thoroughly before using it again.

There is a widespread belief that salt always pulls the paint towards the edges of the stretched out piece of silk, but this is not completely true. This is one explanation for the way in which the streaks form, but it must also depend on how the material was stretched, the direction of the warp and weft threads and whether an outlining agent, such as gutta, has been used. Above all, it depends on how much and how evenly the water has been applied to the area sprinkled with salt.

The illustrations on page 50 show experiments with three different sizes of salt grains. In the left-hand column you can see the beginning of the reaction when salt is scattered on to a freshly-painted area of colour; in the right-hand column, the intermediate stage of the drying process is quite far advanced. The examples on page 48 also clearly show the different effects that can be produced with various types of silk.

Hints on using salt

- The best results are obtained if you can place the grains of salt on the silk individually, as far as possible, spaced out 1–2 cm (½–¾ in).
- Salt must never be allowed to get into the colour containers, as this will cause the paints to thicken and flake off when used.
- If you are planning a piece of work that has some areas with salt effects and some without, it is better to finish all the painting first, without applying salt. Let the silk dry and then wet the areas where salt is required. This is the best way to avoid stains caused by slipping grains of salt.

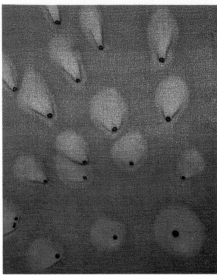
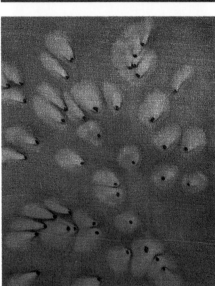

The examples shown here illustrate the beginning (left) and intermediate (right) stages in the reaction caused by salt sprinkled on to wet paint. Three types of salt were used; special salt available for this technique, baking salt and kitchen salt.

special salt

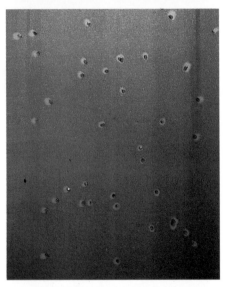

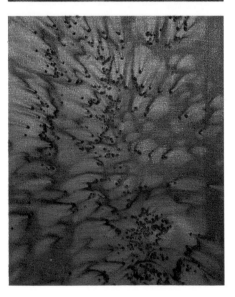

baking salt

kitchen salt

50

Salt experiment

Salt effects can be controlled to some extent if you place a few grains of salt carefully on to *dry* silk and then systematically apply the paint.

You can experiment by using medium grains of salt placed in single or double rows, or in a circle, on to dry, or very slightly damp fabric.

Then, not too quickly, brush on different colours interspersed with a little water. Always work from the same edge along a single row, or through a double row. With a circle, dab paint and water alternately in the centre.

It is important that the paint has plenty of room to spread out into the fabric. If, for example, you paint too near a line of gutta, the colour could be stopped and pushed back again, when too much liquid will collect together. Take your time, because if you apply the paints too quickly, one after another, the excessive wetness can dissolve the grains of salt and reduce the effect. The illustrations on this page show the separation of colours quite clearly.

Circle-shaped arrangement of salt grains.

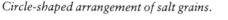

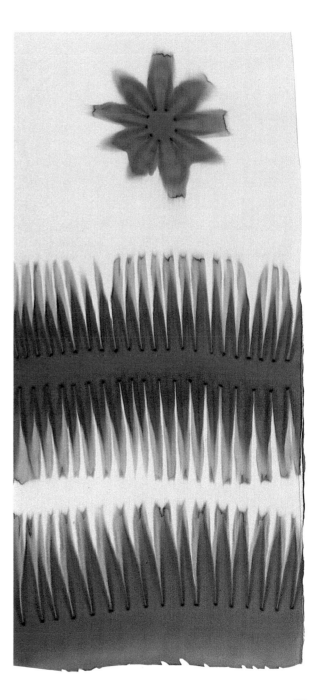

A double row . . . .

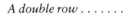

. . . . . . and a single row of salt grains.

In this experiment, medium grains of salt were placed on dry silk, then paint was applied.

Outlining agents

If you want to achieve exact, sharply-defined borders to the areas of colour in your design, without leaving it to chance, you should consider the possibility of using gutta as an outlining agent. An application of this viscous, quick-drying substance limits the spread of colour to the sections defined. With this method you can separate areas from each other, making precise, graphic designs possible.

In batik, hot wax is applied to the fabric with a brush, or Tjanting, (a little can of wax with a spout), to stop liquid colour penetrating, so a 'resist' has been applied to these areas. In silk painting, outlining agents have a similar effect, as they place a barrier around an area where paint is to be applied. Unlike wax, they are heat resistant, which is a definite advantage when fixing the painted silk with hot steam.

The 'gutta' technique is referred to in general, but there are various types of outlining agents on the market with different properties. Basically, they can be divided into water soluble and benzine soluble agents and each has advantages and disadvantages. Because the term 'gutta' is so common, it will be used as a general description of the outlining technique, whether the agents are water or benzine soluble.

A rainy day; this arresting painting is clearly defined with areas of gutta.

52

You can use a brush to apply gutta but it is better to work with a plastic pipette container, which has a small metal nib attached to it. The gutta flows out of a thin slot in the nib and you can choose between different sizes, so the thickness of the outline can be determined beforehand. Applying light pressure to the container, draw the nib across the *dry* silk at an angle of 45°. You will hear the slight scratching noise that the metal nib makes on the silk.

The smoothness of the outline obviously depends on the smoothness of the action. Because all the joining points are visible, and blobs of gutta may occur, it is better to draw each line in one action. It is essential to practice using the pipette on a piece of paper, or an old piece of cloth. Try out the necessary flowing arm and hand movement with a pencil on a large sheet of paper, just to get the feel of the action first.

You can achieve very fine lines by using more viscous gutta, or by working more quickly, but thicker lines require thinner gutta, or drawing the outlines more slowly. The metal nib, with sizes of opening graded from 5–8, controls the amount of gutta that is released. With care and some forethought, the gutta can be matched to the thickness of the material, so that it should be unnecessary to remove any surplus gutta with alcohol or a chemical cleaner. Only experience, however, will enable you to judge the correct relationship between the consistency of the gutta, the thickness of the silk and the speed of application. As a rough guide, fine silk fabrics usually require thin outlines, so the gutta must be more viscous. On thicker silk fabrics, the gutta sinks in so you need broad outlines with thinner gutta.

Water soluble agents	Benzine soluble agents
The outlines must be allowed to dry completely before painting inside the areas. The advantage with this type of agent is that the outlines can be removed from the material by soaking. However, because of the water contained in the paint, the outlines can also sometimes be removed while working on the silk, especially if several layers of colour are applied one on top of another, or spots of colour have been applied too near the outline.	These outlining agents are sold under the name 'gutta', which contains the gelled sap of the gutta-percha tree from south-east Asia, 'Palaquium gutta', a type of rubber plant, or 'serti'. The gutta must be easy-flowing but it will need to be thinned or thickened depending on the thickness of the silk, the width of the visible outline required and on your own individual speed of application. Check with the manufacturer's instructions to see whether you have to let the lines dry before you paint inside the areas. These agents are not removed by normal soaking and you should again follow the manufacturer's instructions.

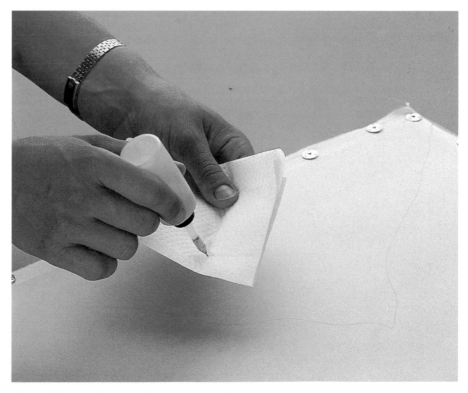

To avoid joining lines, begin the gutta outlines on a piece of paper.

Store gutta containers and nibs in lighter fuel

Because they contain a solvent which evaporates easily, benzine soluble agents should be kept in properly closed containers. The best ones for this purpose are obviously the bottles in which they were purchased, but it is rather time-consuming to squeeze any remaining agent back into the original container each time you use it.

You can avoid the laborious task of cleaning pipette bottles and metal nibs by storing them separately in airtight jars filled with lighter fuel. In the pipette jar the bottles will be so saturated with lighter fuel that the gutta cannot harden. The nibs also clean themselves in the fluid and any stubborn, stuck-on bits of gutta can easily be scraped off with the little pieces of wire that are supplied with the nibs.

Before applying any gutta, you should point the metal nib of the pipette downwards and gently squeeze out any air bubbles, otherwise you will create gaps in your outline and allow paint to seep through. Keep a light pressure on the pipette bottle when you are drawing, so that it does not suck air back in straight away. Have a piece of paper or cloth handy to wipe off the drops of gutta that collect on the nib.

To avoid messy starting points with the gutta, hold a piece of cloth close to the silk and draw a line from the cloth on to the silk, literally without stopping. Blobs of gutta spoil the overall effect of a design and can stick to the paper or iron when you are fixing the paints.

Hints on using gutta
- When painting relatively small areas separated by gutta, begin in the middle of the area. The paint will soak into the silk quickly and run right up to the gutta line. If you begin close to the line, the paint may overflow.
- With large areas separated by gutta, begin your painting on one side and work across to the other side, bit by bit. Any 'stripes' can be well blended in when they are still wet.

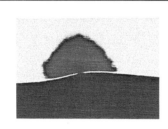

◁ *paint has broken through the line because of an air bubble in the gutta*

there are gaps in the gutta lines, which have been drawn too quickly or inaccurately ▷

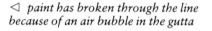

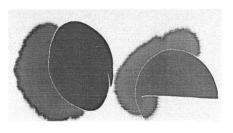

◁ *outlines drawn too quickly or with gutta that was too thick to soak right through the silk*

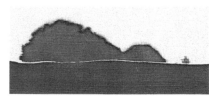

here the outline hasn't been drawn carefully ▷

Rectifying mistakes

When drawing with an outlining agent, inattention or a clumsy movement can cause gaps in the lines. The colour can then seep through these gaps and possibly ruin the whole design. There are subtle ways of disguising these mistakes later on, but it is much better to eliminate any possibility of a mishap by checking everything before you begin.

One problem is caused by little bubbles in the gutta, which are made when thinning and shaking the agent. Sometimes these are so tiny that you cannot see them with the naked eye, especially when using colourless gutta on white silk. You should therefore leave gutta which has just been thinned to stand for a while before it is used.

Gaps which cannot be seen immediately after applying the gutta can be detected more easily if a light is shone through the silk. All outlines that have soaked right through the fabric properly look darker than the surrounding area, or lighter when lit from behind. A more exact, but laborious, method is to cover the areas with clear water, first checking the position of each individual line before the outlined areas are soaked. In this way you can detect any gaps without risk, but remember to dry the silk again before beginning to repair the lines.

In order to remove any colour seepage which may occur, despite all your precautions, begin by filling in the bordering areas with a lighter colour. Allow the colour to dry completely before re-applying the gutta outline, as outlining agents cannot penetrate wet silk. The illustrations on page 54 show a selection of mistakes that often occur in outlines, with their corresponding seepage of colour.

The correct way of removing as much of the colour seepage as possible is explained here, but you cannot do this without leaving some trace of the mistake behind. The worst thing is that perhaps at a place where you wanted a white line in your design, the area will now be coloured where

fig 1: draw over the gap in the line

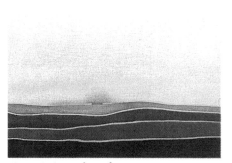

fig 2: lighten the colour run

fig 3: light colour on the area

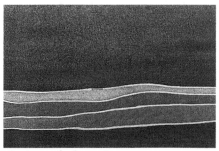

fig 4: use darker paint

the seepage occurred, and has been redrawn with colourless gutta. To disguise this you could perhaps draw a small motif around the error, and repeat this in several other places to balance the design. Unfortunately, not all designs lend themselves to this correction.

Spots of gutta that have accidentally dripped on to the silk present a similar problem. Where possible, they should also be worked into the design, because they can only be partially removed and, even then, they still interfere with the flow of the paint. You can actually see the intentional effect of thinly-spread gutta on page 61.

Correcting mistake

1. Allow the seepage to dry, then draw over the gap with fresh gutta.
2. Lighten the seepage with alcohol; it will be loosened and thinned and some of the colour can be wiped off with a ball of cotton-wool, or some rolled up paper towelling.
3. A light colour cannot always disguise a mistake. You can sometimes still see where the seepage has mixed with the new colour.
4. Only when a darker colour is applied will the seepage almost disappear. It is therefore better to begin the design with a light colour first, so that you don't have to change the colour scheme too much!

Coloured outlines

A wide variety of coloured outlining agents are now available but, as an alternative and to enable you to experiment with this method, you can add enamel paints to benzine soluble gutta, or silk paints to water soluble gutta. However, if you use colours in the gutta which need a fixing agent to make them waterproof, the outlining agent can still lose its colour when washed because it will not be fixed. In effect, with gutta you mix yourself not only are unwanted colours stopped from penetrating the fabric, but it also stops the fixing agent from penetrating, so the colour contained in the outlining agent cannot be fixed in the silk.

The fact that coloured outlines are not always waterproof and that gold, silver and other coloured gutta have a tendency to peel off are problems that have not yet been satisfactorily resolved. There is no doubt, however, that coloured gutta offers wonderful possibilities for work that does not have to be cleaned or washed, such as pictures, but its is less suitable for designs applied to clothing.

Concealed outlines

A very delicate effect can be achieved if you use gutta lines in such a way that when the work is completed, they are no longer visible. To do this you should work with colourless gutta, so that the outlines remain in the colour of the original fabric; white on white unpainted silk, solid colours on silk that has been dyed.

An interesting effect is obtained if the outlined, painted and dried area is made wet again, either with paint or water, as a 'shadow outline' appears on the actual gutta line and forms a dark line that spreads slightly into the area of colour. The line stands out very vividly and seems to push itself into the foreground, with an almost three-dimensional effect. The gutta outline itself is no longer visible and now forms part of the less significant background. After fixing, the gutta outlines can be removed in a benzine bath.

If you use this method, however, you do have the same problem as with coloured outlines, as the paints in the material could be blocked off from the fixative by the gutta. This means that you might not be able to fix the colour under the outlines chemically or by ironing, and it will appear as a lighter shade when the work is finished. If possible, try to steam-fix the fabric instead.

If you use colourless gutta on lightly coloured pre-dyed materials, then all the outlines remain in the original colour. However, some knowledge of the theory of colour is very useful because any colours that are applied to the fabric will mix with the background colour, according to established rules. As an example, you will never be able to achieve a pale yellow when it is applied to a blue background – with this combination the final colour will always be green! Similarly, very dark colours cannot be lightened and you have far more possibilities for experimenting with colour, if you begin with a background in a pale shade.

The illustrations on these two pages show ways in which the techniques described can be used. Further examples of these methods are also shown on pages 89 to 92. If you take your time and experiment you will be delighted, and surprised, by the results you achieve.

Hint for signing designs

– To replace gutta as a means of signing your finished work, metallic pens that can be purchased in office equipment shops are extremely useful. Compared to gold and silver gutta, these dry very quickly and are much easier to write with than a pipette.

– However, they do come off in a benzine bath and this is something to bear in mind on items such as scarves or cushion covers, which will require cleaning. It is the ideal way of signing a framed picture.

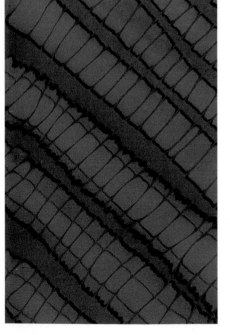

Concealed gutta and colour displacement.

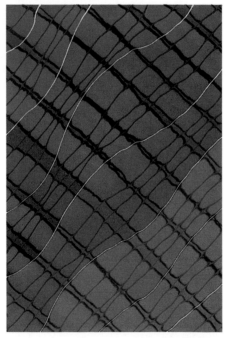

Concealed and visible lines of gutta.

With concealed gutta you can create clear, smooth boundaries without the gutta line itself being visible.

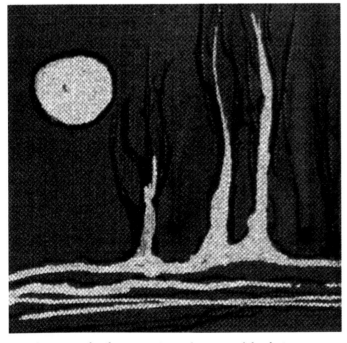

In this example silver gutta is used as part of the design.

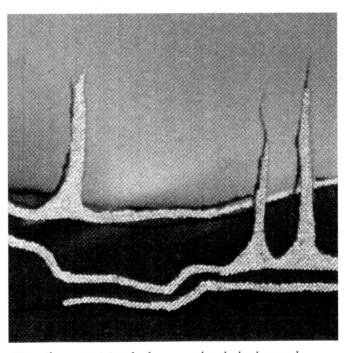

Here silver gutta joins the foreground to the background.

Painting with a hairdryer

Strange as it may seem, an electric hairdryer is useful, although sometimes a little risky, for speeding up the drying of painted silk! With the aid of this tool you can undertake precise work quickly, such as painting wet colours next to dry, or shorten the drying time of background colours and outlining agents.

If you dry an area of wet paint that has been applied next to a dry one very rapidly, you achieve quite a smooth outline. You get a similar effect with alcohol which naturally evaporates and dries quickly. With a hairdryer, however, you can fix a colour that has only lightly soaked into the material, or water that you have applied to a certain area, and the shape of the area will not change, as would be the case during a normally long drying period.

Although it is virtually impossible to create an outline which just disappears into thin air with this method, you can use it to make part of the area of colour dry more quickly. In this way you achieve a very smooth transition between the dry and wet area. If you then apply paint to both areas at the same time, it will be drawn into the wet area and, in doing so, will create an outline against the dry area. In the transition zone between the wet and dry areas, the colour becomes gradually less obvious until it has completely disappeared. In landscape painting, this can become one of the most crucial elements in the design. It immediately creates an impression of mist or fog

Painting with the h

and gives the pi
depth.

The danger of
that you can un place
dried outlines where you don't want
them! This is difficult to avoid,
especially when you first begin to

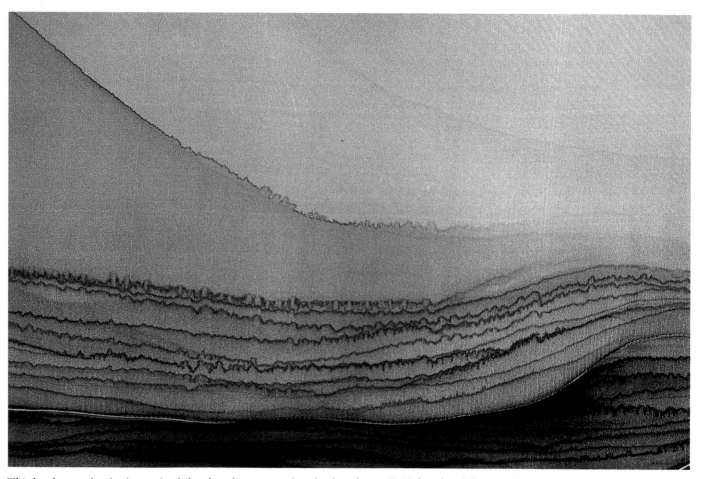

*This landscape clearly shows the defined outlines created with a hairdryer. (S. Hahn, detail from **Midday**.)*

experiment. The hairdryer should be on a setting that is neither too hot nor too strong, and it should not be held too close to the silk or the brush, otherwise the gutta or the silk itself might become discoloured, or even burnt by the heat. Also, if you use too much heat, the colour can sometimes change, or dry unevenly and in patches. If the stream of air is too strong, then freshly-applied alcohol and water, as well as paint, can be blown to one side and will collect in small puddles on the silk, and leave behind shapeless lines.

Obviously, you cannot use salt effects and a hairdryer together at the same time. The salt would be moved from the area where it was supposed to be creating an effect and leave unwanted tracks. Also, the salt has to be allowed to dry slowly to achieve a complete reaction.

The illustration, bottom right, shows how you can freeze colours in quite distinct outlines with a hairdryer. The colours were applied in layers, getting darker each time. Finally, spots of paint, water and alcohol were applied to enliven the monotony of the stripes. The woodgrain effect is for more advanced silk painters.

This woodgrain pattern has been achieved with the help of a hairdryer.

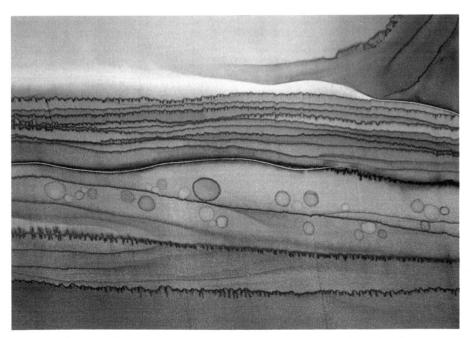

Edges made with a hairdryer, gutta lines and spots of alcohol are all used in this painting.

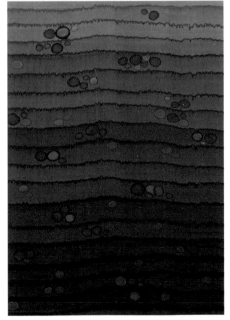

An experiment working from light to dark tones.

Impregnated backgrounds

In the silk painting techniques given so far, emphasis has been placed on the particularly good flowing properties of the paints and how to make the most of this characteristic. However, you might eventually want to prevent this flowing of colour to achieve a more robust background, and you can apply various types of finish to the silk to limit the spread of the paints.

Three possibilities are given here and you should experiment to see which gives you the best results. The effects you have achieved with the salt technique may well lead you to try a salt impregnated background, or your experiences with gutta to try a mixture of gutta and benzine. You can also purchase antifusant solutions from various paint manufacturers, which can be brushed on to the silk over large areas, or in patches, before painting, to alter and reduce the flowing capacity of the paints.

A salt background has been used for this landscape.

Salt impregnation

For a salt solution, the basic ingredients are as follows:

250gm (9oz) cooking salt.
1 litre (1¾ pints) warm water.
Sprinkle the salt into the water and stir in until it has all more or less dissolved. Leave for about an hour, then filter the solution to remove any undissolved crystals.

Brush this solution on to the silk, with some added colour if you want to add a tone to the background, then leave the silk to dry completely. The effect comes from the salt which recrystallizes as it dries and forms a barrier in the silk which resists the penetration of paint. The results are never exactly the same, because the way in which the salt dries influences the colours. If the background dries slowly in a cold environment, large salt crystals are formed. With quick drying, accelerated with a hairdryer if necessary, the crystals are smaller and more finely distributed over the silk. When dry, you can paint over the area.

A rhythmic pattern in tones of blue.

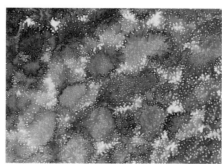

Alternating bright and dull shapes.

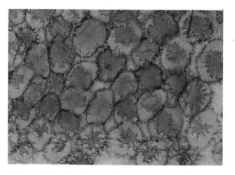

Here mixed colours have split up.

The examples shown here illustrate the very grainy patterns, or smooth areas which are achieved. In places you can clearly see how the mixed paints have split up into their components, with the freer-flowing pigments spreading out more quickly. As explained in the salt technique on page 48, mixed colours often split up in this way. To achieve further effects on an impregnated background and painted area, alcohol works better than water.

Mixed colours on a salt background.

Gutta and benzine impregnation

Another method, which limits the spread of paint on silk more effectively than salt impregnation, is a gutta and benzine background. The basic ingredients are as follows:

5ml (¼ fluid oz) gutta.
95ml (3½ fluid oz) washing or cleaning benzine, such as lighter fuel. Dissolve the gutta in the benzine, noting that the proportions should not differ too much, otherwise the impregnation will not reduce the flowing properties of the paint at all, or it will make the paint peel off the silk completely.

Spread a thin layer of the gutta background over the whole area; this has a similar controlling effect as gutta lines. The benzine is a solvent that evaporates, so it dries quickly and you can soon begin to paint on the background. The silk now behaves like unabsorbent paper and you can paint very fine lines and details, such as the branches of a tree.

It opens up even greater possibilities if you want to consider using spraying equipment, such as fixative sprayers, perfume atomisers or spray guns, to apply paint to the background. The colours will stay exactly where you spray them and completely new shapes can be created with stencils. Inside dampened areas you can paint soft shades of colour just as with silk that has not been impregnated. Watercolour and salt techniques can also be used on silk with a gutta and benzine background.

Antifusant impregnation

Some paint manufacturers offer solvents in addition to their range of colours, and these limit the flow of the paints. Although originally intended for mixing with individual colours, these can be used as a background impregnation. Follow the manufacturer's instructions and experiment to see what effects you can obtain.

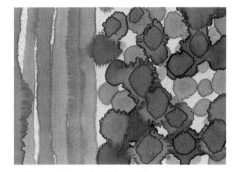

Colours thinned with antifusant.

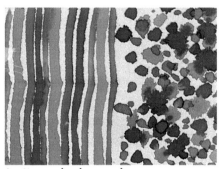

Antifusant background.

Impregnation makes fine lines possible.

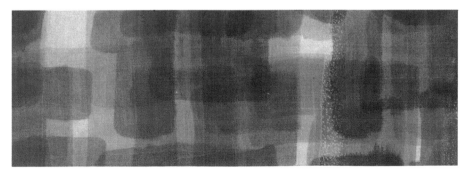

A transparent effect is created on a fine salt background.

Steam-fixing

Unfixed painted silk is very receptive to light and humidity, but certain processes make it washable and ensure that it does not fade. Fixing the paint with an iron or with a chemical agent has been described on pages 33–34, but the best results and most brilliant colours are achieved by steam-setting.

Comprehensive details of the equipment needed for steam-fixing and step-by-step instructions are given on the following pages. The use of a domestic pressure cooker is compared with a professional steamer, and the advantages and disadvantages of each method are outlined. At first glance, this method of fixing may appear rather complicated but it is well worth the extra effort to obtain satisfactory results.

With steam-fixing it is possible to set more than one piece of work at a time, so it can be economical if you intend to produce several designs. Each piece, however, must be kept separate from the others, as the colours will mix with one another if they are allowed to come into contact. The piece of silk should be rolled up in a single or, preferably, double layer of absorbent paper and placed in hot steam for about 45–60 minutes.

Equipment
– Pressure cooker, 5 or 7 litres (8¾ or 12¼ pint) capacity.
– Deep inner steamer.
– Newspaper for lining.
– Tripod to raise the steamer off the bottom of the cooker.
– Paper waste, or newspapers at least 6 weeks old, in which to roll up the silk that is being fixed.
– Plastic adhesive tape to secure the rolls of paper.
– Aluminium foil to protect the silk. 200–300ml (7–10½ fluid oz) water, depending on the size of cooker.

– Heat source, gas stove or electric ring.
– Wooden or metal ruler for tearing the silk and scissors for cutting.

Pressure cooker

The advantage of this inexpensive method is that the equipment you require can usually be found in any household.

The disadvantages are that the capacity of the cooker will only allow about 2 square metres (2 square yards) of fabric to be fixed. Also, creases cannot always be completely ironed out. The most persistent problem, however, is that condensation drips on to the rolled up silk and this causes light-coloured stains, but there is a way of overcoming this.

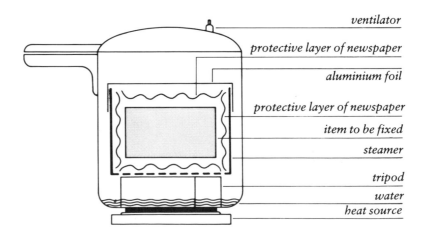

ventilator
protective layer of newspaper
aluminium foil
protective layer of newspaper
item to be fixed
steamer
tripod
water
heat source

1. If you have used salt, make sure that you have removed it all, then lay the dry silk on the newpaper. Use the ruler to tear off the excess silk; about 5cm (2in) on each side and 10cm (4in) at the top and bottom.

2. Roll up the item in the paper so that no part of the silk comes into contact with another. Avoid creases and make sure that the silk does not extend beyond the paper. Any holes in the paper will cause staining that will spoil the end result.

3. Secure the paper roll with plastic adhesive tape, because paper tape will not stand up to the fixing temperature. Roll up each item *separately*.

4. Line the base and sides of the inner steamer with a thick layer of newspaper.

5. Place the rolled up piece of silk in a spiral shape inside the lined steamer.

6. Place a thick layer of newspaper on top of the steamer to protect the silk from condensation.

7. As an additional protection against drops of condensation that fall from the lid of the cooker, mould aluminium foil around the edges of the steamer, so that any drops run outside the steamer, and not into it.

8. Pour the water into the cooker, to a depth of 1–2cm (½–¾ in). Place the tripod and steamer in the cooker. On heat setting 2, the fixing process takes about 45 minutes. Leave the cooker to cool until the ventilator has subsided before opening.

9. Although the paint manufacturer may recommend that you do not wash the silk for 2–4 hours, the best way to get rid of any creases is to wash the silk immediately and then iron it dry, see page 34.

Professional steam-fixing

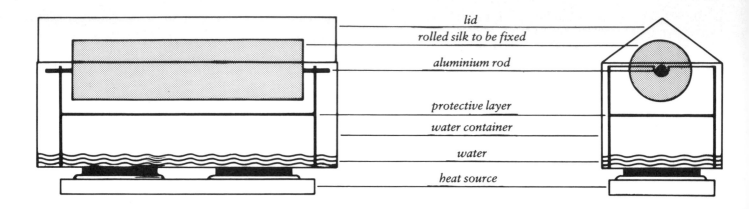

lid
rolled silk to be fixed
aluminium rod

protective layer
water container
water
heat source

If you intend to give courses on silk painting, or produce valuable designs for sale, suitable professional fixing equipment is available. Although this is fairly expensive, it can fix up to 18 continuous metres (yards) of silk at a time in about 60 minutes, depending on the thickness of the fabric and the number of layers of paper. Specialist shops will be pleased to give you further information.

1. This type of professional fixing equipment requires the water container, a protective layer, an aluminium rod and the lid. The only other materials you need are waste paper or newspaper, plastic adhesive tape, water and a heat source, for example, two electric rings side-by-side.

2. Roll the piece of silk at its full width on to the aluminium rod, with one or two layers of waste paper between. Make sure the paper extends beyond both side edges of the fabric. When all the pieces of silk have been wrapped separately in this way, cover the rolls with 3–5 more pieces of paper, to protect the items against any possible drops of condensation. Fasten the paper with a few strips of plastic adhesive tape.

3. Place the water container over two gas burners or two electric rings. Pour water in to a depth of 2cm (¾ in). Place the protective layer into the water container and lay the silk to be fixed in the slot in the protective layer.

4. Put the lid on the apparatus and set the heat source fairly high at first, until steam escapes, then reduce the heat. From this point the fixing process takes about 45–60 minutes, depending on the thickness of the roll.

When the fixing process is completed, remove the lid, taking care that you are not scalded by the rising steam. Let the roll cool off for a further 10–15 minutes before you unpack the fixed pieces of silk and hang them up to dry. For hints on washing, see page 30.

The theory of colour

Although we could quite easily cope in a world without colour and with which we are, to some extent, already familiar from black-and-white films, colour enriches our entire lives. It also tells us a great deal about the nature of things around us; it can warn us, catch our attention, and influence our feelings. The more conscious we are of colour, the more interesting and evocative our designs will be, as we experiment with their effect on our work. The following pages will help you to discover your sense of colour, so that the composition of different colour tones will no longer seem a mystery. Don't just read these pages, however, but take a brush and the three primary colours, red, blue and yellow, thinned with the normal amount of alcohol and water, and become involved ·in the world of colour.

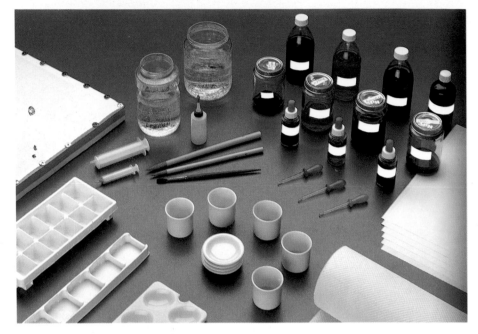

Equipment for colour mixing experiments. A sufficient number of mixing jars is vital.

When you consider the phenomenon of colour in more depth, you will realise that there isn't actually such a thing as pure objective 'colour'. What we perceive is really an effect produced by light waves when they pass through the eye and fall on the retina, sending impulses from there to the brain. The sun's rays contain a range of electromagnetic waves, which we receive in the following way according to their wavelengths; we perceive the longest waves as red and after that orange, yellow, green, blue, until the shortest wave, which we register as violet.

In this range of violet colour, progressively less and less white light is reflected.

Some reptiles and insects, such as snakes and bees, can distinguish other colours within this range. Sunlight, which we perceive as white, actually contains the whole range of waves.

So why, then, does a red flower look red? The answer lies quite simply in the composition of the flower and its pigments. It can absorb part of the light falling on it, but reflects the remainder. It is the reflected part that falls on our retina and, in this case, is seen by us as red. A black box, however, reflects hardly anything as it absorbs all the light, so there is no reflection to create the impression of colour in our brain. Black is therefore a 'non-colour'. White is also a 'non-colour' but, in this case, it reflects all the light so that no wavelength is able to dominate and create a sense of colour.

Johannes Itten's colour circle.

A comparison of shades of red and blue produced by different manufacturers.

The effect that the process of light absorption and reflection has during painting is illustrated by the range of violet tones on page 66. More and more layers of light violet were painted on to white silk but the silk ceases to reflect all the light, because the pigments absorb the yellow and only reflect the violet. The more pigment you put on the silk, the more is taken away from the light; this is called 'colour subtraction', because the intensity of the light is taken away. If, on the other hand, you were to shine several violet spotlights on to a white wall, this spot would become lighter and lighter, or 'colour addition'.

In silk painting we are dealing with colour subtraction. This means that, for example, you could not paint with yellow on black silk, because the light that is necessary for the yellow could not reach it. The effect is different with oil colours, however, and with all covering paints, as the new colour will simply cover up the layer of colour below it.

The enormous variation in colours has been investigated by many people because, above all, they wanted to introduce some sense of order into the world of colour. Johannes Itten created a working hypothesis with his 'colour circle', which is a useful aid for understanding the mixing of colours. It begins in the centre of the circle with the three primary colours, which cannot be mixed from any other colours; red, yellow and blue. If you take two of these colours and mix the same amounts of each together,

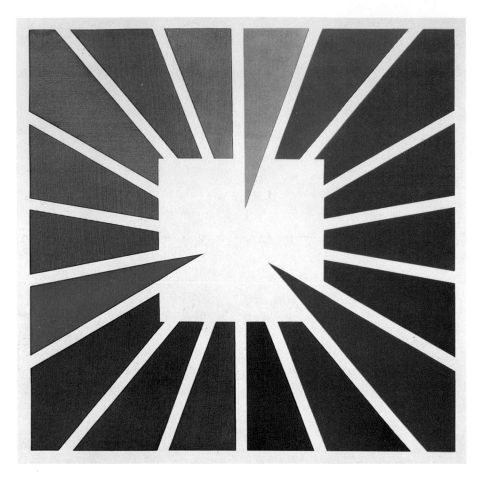

A mixing experiment of 18 colours, obtained with mathematical proportions of red, blue and yellow.

should always begin with the lighter one and carefully introduce the darker one. If you mix them the other way round, you may end up using far too much of the light colour to produce the tone you want.

It will help if you try mixing your colours according to the tables on these two pages, so that you get used to the colour circle. The fact that yellow is the weakest primary colour has been taken into account but instead of doubling the amount of yellow, you can also halve the red or blue – it is the ratio that is important. From the original three primary colours, 33 graduated tones can be mixed and if you then arrange your results in a circle, you can construct your own 36-section wheel. In addition to these you can produce brown and grey as already explained, and you can darken each colour with black, or lighten them by thinning them, so that more of the white silk shines through.

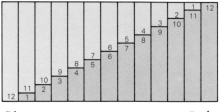

Blue   *Red*

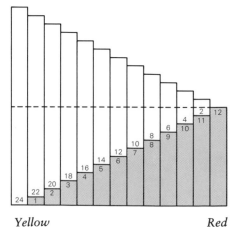

Yellow   *Red*

you get three related colours; orange, green and violet. Putting all these together, you already have a colour circle with six sections. If you continue mixing these three newly-created secondary colours with their original primary colours, to arrive at intermediate colours, a circle with twelve sections is created. You can continue this process until you can scarcely detect any difference at all between each step, at about 48 colours. So a circle of adjacent colours is formed, but if you mix together a secondary colour with the opposite primary colour, a brown or greyish colour is created. Colours that lie directly opposite each other in the circle, or complementary colours, will produce a neutral grey when mixed together.

This mixing can only be done exactly if really perfect base colours are used, which is virtually impossible. Generally, almost all makes of paint differ from the ideal colour, as you can see from the collection of silk painting colours shown on page 67. It must also be admitted that we all see colour differently!

The 18–step experiment in colour mixing on this page shows another phenomenon; when mixing in the same mathematically exact proportions of yellow, it will hardly alter the neighbouring blue or red, but steps are created in the sequence of the circle. Not only does yellow have different colour characteristics to red or blue but, quite clearly, the contrast in lightness is crucial. Therefore, if you want to mix a medium light orange from red and yellow, you must add a greater amount of yellow than red, so that the red is actually lightened. When mixing colours you

When using colours you must always take into account the fact that they never create an effect on their own, as they are always influenced by their surroundings, so that tension, harmony and disharmony occur. We react to various colours by comparing their contrasting brightness, the size of the area of colour, and the different intensities. Complementary colours that lie opposite each other in the colour circle become brighter when placed next to each other and the eye can even strengthen the colour when used on its own. For example, neutral grey can produce a different effect depending on the surrounding colour, and it seems to take on some of the complementary colour. Similarly, if you stare at a red square surrounded by white and then, after some time, close your eyes, a green after-image appears.

In the scarf design shown here, you can see how the different contrasts have been created. Our eyes see the greatest difference in colour tone between the blue and the red, and the areas show marked degrees of brightness. The bright red, a warm colour, seems to leap forward into the foreground, compared to the cold blue and darker tones. You should always bear this in mind when painting landscapes, because you can use it to create an impression of perspective. You will also observe that the bright red only needs a small area, because it has much greater intensity than its surroundings. This positioning of colour is always most important in creating the effect you have in mind.

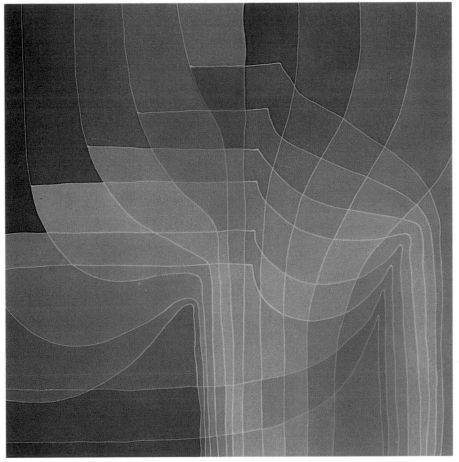

A scarf painted in blues and reds.

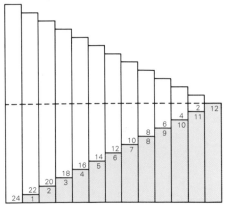

Yellow   Blue

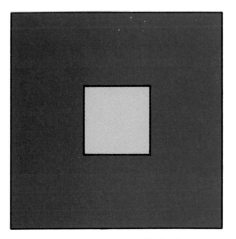

Simultaneous contrast, which always influences our sight, is based on the fact that colours are never isolated from their surroundings. This phenomenon is often demonstrated by using two squares.

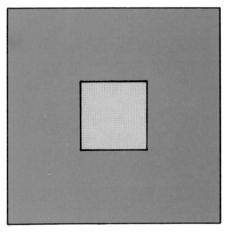

Both inner squares are the same grey, but you usually get the impression that the grey in the red area seems a little green, and the grey in the green area slightly red. Your eyes and brain have supplied these colours.

Sources of inspiration

People often ask the question, 'Can someone without any talent for drawing try silk painting?', but anyone who feels uncertain about their ability can, with clear instructions and a little understanding of colour, produce exciting designs. It does not depend on an extensive knowledge of perspective and proportion, as silk painting is a technique in which the particular flowing properties of the paints can easily form lively and original effects. Experimenting with colours, by blending and contrasting them, is very important and you should spend some time studying the theory of colour, see pages 66–69. This will improve your sense of colour and you will be more conscious of the way they relate to each other.

Silk painting is certainly not an art, or craft, that can be undertaken at great speed! One of the most important requirements is patience and being able to work in peace without pressure, preferably in a place where you can leave a design you have begun for quite long periods of time. Clearly, if you have been concentrating on painting for several hours, a break from it will give you time to consider what you have produced so far and assess how the design is developing. Becoming too immersed in painting seldom results in success, as you tend to miss the natural point at which you should stop and end up doing too much, so that the design becomes cluttered.

Unfortunately, we lose most of our childhood spontaneity and creativity as we grow older, and self-criticism increases. Too much detailed pre-planning and striving for fixed ideas, however, will only cramp your style, which is why you should always experiment with colours, techniques and fabrics. You will often obtain quite unexpected results, but because they have been created unintentionally, they will have a lively and unique effect. Complete beginners should not rigidly follow instructions, but should

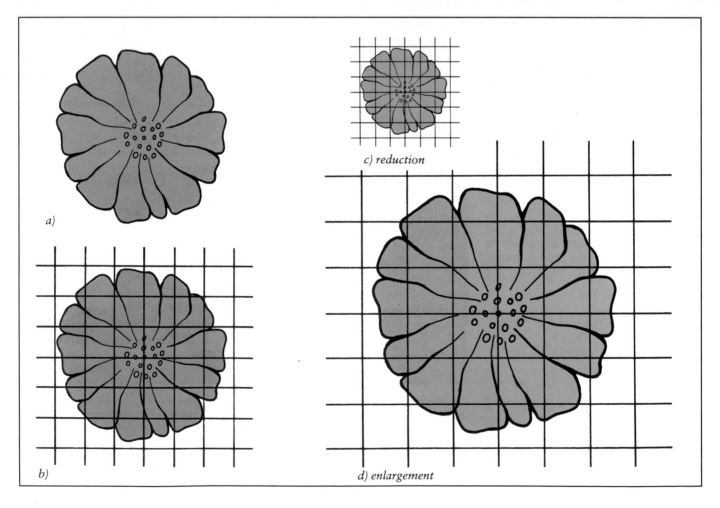

a)

b)

c) reduction

d) enlargement

keep their eyes and mind open, so that they do not miss these happy moments of chance!

You will achieve much more from this original painting technique if you are always prepared to revise your ideas, whether they are just a glimmer in your mind, or in sketch form. If you confine yourself too much you may run the risk of final disappointment at the stilted effect you have produced. There are various ways of coming up with original and attractive designs and you should take some time to explore these. Some people prefer not to begin with any fixed idea, but merely play with colours that reflect their mood at the time and let them run into each other. Others begin by laying down a pattern of lines on the silk with gutta. With both these methods, you can gradually build up a design until you are satisfied with the results. This is when it helps to go away and think about your painting.

Other people don't trust their own ability at all and resort to pattern templates, or stencils. With this method, the design is reproduced exactly and the colours applied without variation. Between these two extremes lies the possibility of looking for ideas in your daily surroundings, colour schemes in nature or the outlines of flowers, and transferring the idea into silk painting.

Often a sketch you have seen, or even a design in this book, cannot be transferred directly on to silk, because it is either too large or too small for your purpose. This is not too much of a problem, however, as the size of most designs can be changed by reducing or enlarging them on a photocopier.

Another method can also be adopted but this requires some patience. To enlarge a design, place a piece of paper divided into squares over the original design, and number the squares both horizontally and vertically to produce a grid. Now take a piece of paper to the size of the design you require and divide and number this in the same way. Study

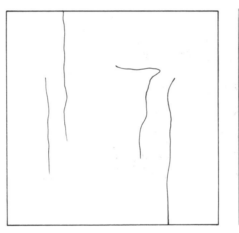

1. *Cell structure of an elm tree.*

2. *From photograph to sketch.*

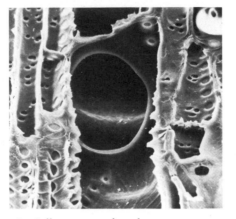

3. *Design for gutta outlines.*

4. **Elmwood**, *painted and machine-stitched.*

each small square of the drawing and reproduce the lines in the same position and to the correct proportions in the larger square of your pattern. When all the lines have been transferred, even out any irregularities along the dividing lines of each square. To reduce a design, reverse this procedure to obtain a smaller drawing.

To transfer the sketch on to the silk, lay the fabric over the pattern and trace the lines which can be seen through it with a soft pencil. With this method, the pencil lines cannot be removed later, so you will need to cover them with gutta outlines. As an alternative, trace over the outlines on the paper with a thick, black felt-tipped pen and lay this on the table, under the stretched out silk in the

frame. If you are using ponge silk, the lines should show up even though there is a gap between the sketch and the silk. Look at each individual line and transfer them, bit by bit, directly on to the silk with gutta. The most important thing is to keep your eye on the gutta lines, only glancing at the sketch, otherwise the outlines will be shaky and have gaps in them.

You will find your work less cramped, however, if you lay the sketch next to the stretched out piece of silk and transfer the outlines freehand. The design will reflect your style and panache. The sequence from photographic idea to sketch, and from gutta lines to the finished design is illustrated on this page. This painting is entitled 'Elmwood', and the picture is shown on page 97.

71

Design suggestions

An artistic design does not mean that a subject must be represented exactly true to life in a certain technique, such as silk painting. Even a photograph is an abstraction, because it cannot reproduce the three-dimensions of the original theme. Very often, only a distinct part of the reality is of interest, or a single aspect. The concentric rhythm of a circular staircase, or an electricity pylon can be fascinating.

Tracks left behind on the beach produce a natural rhythm, however, and you will discover many exciting shapes caused by the continuous effects of wind and water. The annual rings in wood also create a contrast with the shells of small sea creatures, and the growth of knots has created radiating calluses.

72

As well as graphic elements in nature, colours obviously evoke an atmosphere. The colours and contours of the clouds in the sky, the distant moutains and the water, all create a harmonious effect. In contrast, the flower leaps forward from its green surrounding. The brightness of the colours has been enhanced by comparison, because they are placed so close to each other. In both instances, the effects are striking.

Don't limit yourself to finding inspiration only in nature, flowers and animals. Even machines, or building sites, have interesting details. In the illustration here, the colour contrasts are heightened by straight lines that form a circle, and the delicate patterns that shine through and add a new dimension.

A strong contrast with sharp outlines has been created by back-lighting.

A slatted wooden wall has a weathered appearance that catches the eye.

You obtain a different perspective of everyday items if you approach them more closely, even going down to ground level. Here the shape and colour of nasturtium seeds inspired a photograph.

Making beautiful
painted silk designs

Suggestions for silk designs

This section suggests ways of using painted silk, to present your work in the best possible way. One great advantage of this painting medium is that your don't only have to use it for pictures. It is a beautiful textile and can be made into many useful and desirable designs, from something as tiny as a brooch to a long, flowing evening dress.

Brooches

These can easily be made from printed off-cuts, or pieces used for experiments, which are often full of interesting little shapes.

Materials

Any type of silk is suitable, except wild silk, as you cannot achieve the delicate textures and minature designs that are associated with brooches with this fabric.

You can use any colour or design you like. Two alternative methods of making brooches are given, both relying on adhesives rather than on being drawn together at the back with stitches, which is usually recommended. This method is rather bulky.

You can use brooch mountings that are readily available in craft shops. Belt buckles and lockets can also be completed in this way.

Method A: This requires a 3-piece brooch mounting, painted silk, self-adhesive card, pair of pliers, scissors and pencil.

Method B: This requires a 2-piece brooch mounting, painted silk, white card with brooch-sized hole cut out, double-sided adhesive tape, pencil, scissors and glue.

Method A

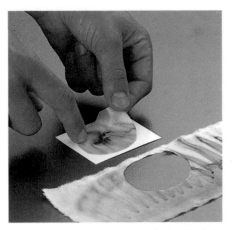

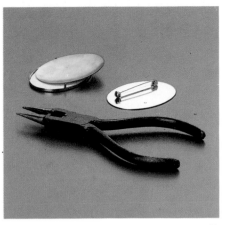

1. Choose your design by moving the brooch frame over the fabric until you have found an attractive motif.

2. Cut out the piece of fabric, slightly larger than the frame, and place it on the self-adhesive card. Lay the slightly curved middle section on top of it, draw round it exactly with a pencil and then cut out the piece of card just inside the line.

3. Assemble the card with the silk painting attached, the middle section, and the back with the brooch fastening. Use the pliers to bend the metal clips into place.

Method B

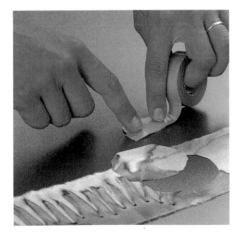

1. Choose your design by moving the piece of white card with the hole cut out of it over the fabric until you have found an attractive motif. Cut the material out, leaving an allowance. Cover both sides of the middle section with double-sided tape and cut off any extra right up to the metal edge.

2. Attach the piece of silk to the sticky surface of the tape and trim the edge to 5 mm (¼ in). Press the edge down on the reverse side.

3. Place some glue around the edge of the brooch frame and press the middle section in, taking care not to let any glue ooze out!

Greetings cards

A greetings card mounted with hand-painted silk makes an attractive gift. You can either cut some card to size yourself, or choose from the mounts that are available from craft shops. These come in various colours and formats, rectangular, round or oval, and usually come complete with a matching envelope. Self-adhesive card is useful for attaching the silk to the card and you will need a pair of scissors. Glue also comes in handy but should only be used sparingly.

Any type of silk is suitable, although slubbed silk does not allow fine details in what is, in effect, a painted miniature. You can section a piece of silk into areas and paint definite designs on it, or look through your off-cuts and experimental pieces for suitable motifs. Because these designs will not be rubbed, or washed, all kinds of techniques are possible. Gold and silver gutta, or metallic pens can be used to produce wonderful effects but before you begin to mark the silk, remember to fix it!

The easiest way of mounting your design is to tear the motif from the silk, so that the edges are frayed all round and then stick it straight on to the card with double-sided adhesive tape. Do not use glue as this will sink through the fabric and mark it.

With what are called 'passepartout' cards, a picture-sized window has already been cut out and you position your design behind this. Attach the silk to a piece of self-adhesive card and place it behind the window. A single piece of card normally comes with a double card, and this can be stuck on the back of your motif to neaten it. You can sign your design on the front of the card and it's all ready for posting!

The illustrations below show how

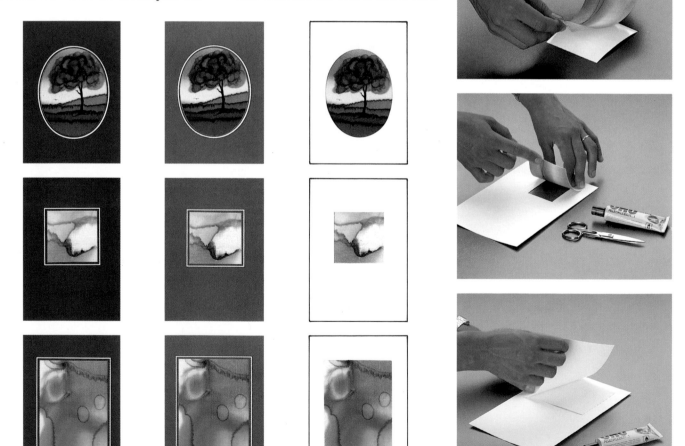

78

the colour of the card can effect the overall impression of the design. The same design is used in three different mounts to show the comparison.

Silk pictures

The next step from making a greetings card is to decorate your walls with your own original pictures. This is simply a card with a picture-sized window, with an area of mount all round to allow sufficient space between the painting fixed behind it and its surroundings. If the colours of the design and card are well-matched, then the effect is greatly enhanced and the examples on the previous page show how important this is. The shape and size of the window will also influence the overall effect. Sometimes the decorations of the room where the picture will be displayed must be taken into account, as the colours of the wall, carpet and furnishings must all be in harmony with the painting.

It is not at all difficult to frame a picture yourself. Many art and craft shops stock suitable card for making the mount in a variety of colours.

Materials

- Card of a colour that enhances the painting.
- Paperknife.
- Large piece of cardboard as a cutting board.
- Metal rule as a cutting guide.
- Ruler for measurements.
- Suitable frame, or frameless picture holder.

Method

Before cutting the card, bear in mind that the greater the width of the mount, the more the painting will be shown to advantage, so don't cut it too narrow. It is also better to choose the optical centrepoint of the card, which always lies somewhere slightly above the mathematical one. Unfortunately, in ready-made mounts, this point is always exactly in the middle and the reason for this is commercial – the purchaser can then either use it horizontally or vertically. With an optical centre-point, the gap between the bottom edge of the card and the painting is greater than that between the top edge of the picture and the card. With very large pictures the difference can amount to a few centimetres (inches), but there is no precise formula – simply judge it the way you see it.

At the same time as you purchase the card, obtain a suitable frame and transfer the measurements of the frame to the card. Make some test cuts on a spare piece of card until you have a feel for the metal cutting guide and the paperknife, then cut the outside edge of the card to size. Make sure you keep to a distinct line and do not cut past a point that you have decided beforehand.

Measure the area of the painting which you wish to display – you don't have to cut off any rough edges as they will be hidden behind the mount. As soon as you have decided whether you want a horizontal or vertical picture, you can begin to work out the size of window you will require. On the reverse side of the mount, pencil in the shape of the window. Lay the card on the cutting board and place the metal cutting guide flush

with one of the lines. Using the paperknife, cut from one corner to the other. The sharpness of the knife and the angle at which you draw it across the card will determine the neatness of the cut. A slanting, or bevelled cut is particularly elegant but is a little more difficult. You can purchase a ready-made mount, or an art shop will undertake this finish for you. A fine line round the window on the mount adds the final touch.

Now you only need to position your silk painting, which can be mounted on self-adhesive card, or remain unmounted. Attach it behind the cut-out window with adhesive tape and it is ready for framing.

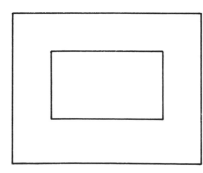
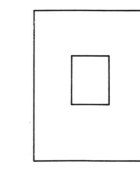

On all rectangular picture formats, the bottom edge of the mount should always be a bit wider than the top edge.

Framing

The overall effect of your finished silk picture will obviously be enhanced by the mount and the way in which it is framed, so it is worth giving careful consideration to the art of presentation.

The most inexpensive way is to make your own frame and wooden laths for frames can be purchased in most DIY stores, in assorted sizes and colours. You can have them cut to size with mitred joints and with the help of some wood glue, your frame will soon be completed.

For a very simple wallhanging, you will need four flat strips of wood. These should be the width of the silk to be framed, plus an allowance of 2cm (¾ in) overhang at each end. If you wish to varnish or paint these, do so before attaching them to the silk, and leave them to dry.

Turn in the side edges of your silk and neaten them It is often a good idea to fix a piece of white cloth to the back. Tear the top and bottom edges of the silk straight across and glue the strip of wood to the back and front of the lower edge. If you wish to hang the picture on a cord, insert a strong piece of twine between the two top strips and glue them in position.

Another way of displaying your silk picture without putting glass in front of it, is to mount it on a wooden board, or artist's stretcher. Edge your piece of silk all the way round with strips of strong material, such as cotton calico, in a suitable colour. Place some interfacing between the silk and the board, stretch it out and tack it down. If you stretch the silk while it is wet, it will smooth itself out and tighten up while it is drying. Depending on the width of the strip

of cloth, you will create an impression of a mount or frame.

If you do not mind if your painting has a few ripples here and there, because of room temperature and humidity, then you can fray about 5mm (¼ in) around all the edges once it has been torn to the correct size, and stick the top edge only on to a suitable card background. Don't forget to take the optical centrepoint into consideration. This can now be placed into a frameless picture holder and held together with metal clips.

You can also adopt the greetings card method of positioning the painting on self-adhesive card, or lampshade card, see page 83. This explains how to attach the silk to the card without making any creases.

If you want the best possible finish for your picture, however, you can purchase ready-made frames, complete with surround, glass, backing and fixtures, from most art shops. These come in all shapes, sizes and finishes and the shop will probably be able to frame your work for you.

The top and bottom of a wallhanging are held between the strips of wood.

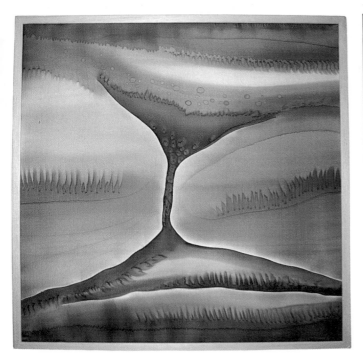

Above: A wooden frame without glass and next to it, with glass and mount.
Right: A painting backed with interfacing and with a fabric mount, is fixed to a wooden board.
Below: Frameless picture holder and a bevelled mount made from strong card.

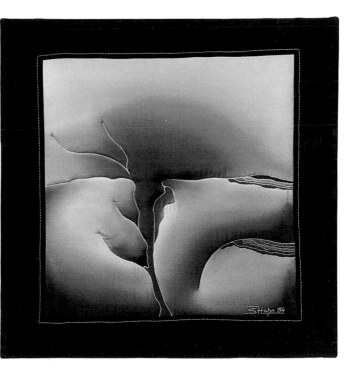

Lampshades

Most craft shops sell self-adhesive lampshade card and a wide selection of lampshade rings. It is best to seek their advice on the type and size most suitable for your requirements, as the diameter of the ring depends on the height of the lampshade and, obviously, on the size of your silk painting. Wait until you have obtained all the necessary equipment, before you measure out and paint the silk.

The mathematical equation for finding the circumference of a circle or, in this case, of the lampshade ring is $2 \times$ pi $(\pi) \times$ radius, or diameter $\times$ pi (π), (pi $= 3.14$ constant ratio). As the rings are seldom the same size, however, and calculations for oval or odd-shaped rings are considerably more difficult, the simplest and safest way is to roll the ring along in a straight line. Mark a spot on a strip of wood, or on the floor. Place the join of the lampshade ring on this spot and then roll it around until you reach the join again. Mark where it finishes and measure the distance it has travelled. This gives you the exact length measurement of the silk, or the complete circumference. The width measurement of the silk will give you the height of the finished lampshade. When you paint the silk, leave an allowance of 3cm (1¼ in) all round it, i.e. 6cm (2½ in) extra on the length and width, for fixing.

Hints on making lampshades

- Yellow, orange, red and brown give a warm light; blue and green tones give a cold one.
- On round shades don't place the design too far to one side, or the join will interfere with it.
- With oval shades, place the join on one of the shallow bends, so that the shade can show two uninterrupted broad sides.

A silk lampshade that matches your furnishings is not difficult to make.

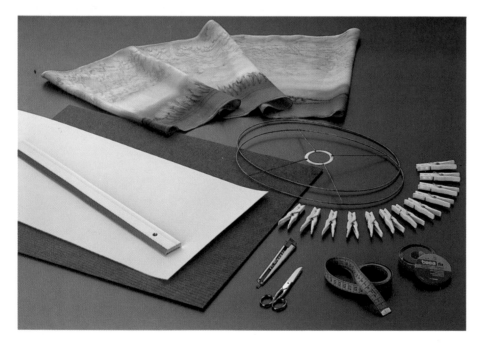

Materials

- 2 lampshade rings, one with a support.
- Painted silk, not too thin; length, circumference of ring + 6cm (2½ in), width, height of lampshade + 6cm (2½ in).
- Lampshade card; length, circumference of ring + 1cm (½ in) overlap, width, height of shade.
- Metal rule, tape measure.
- Scissors, paper or carpet knife.
- Cutting board.
- Double-sided adhesive tape.
- Clothes pegs.

Method

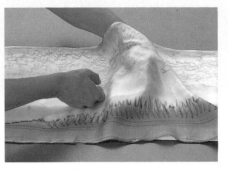

1. Cut the self-adhesive card to the correct size, by running a paper-knife along the metal rule. Lay the card out in front of you with the protective film uppermost and the silk on top of this. Fold the fabric back a bit, so that you can peel the protective film back by about 5cm (2in). Stick the end of the silk down, so that there is an allowance of 3cm (1¼ in) on all sides.

2. Gradually peel back the protective film from under the fabric, so that the silk is stuck down on the card. Creases can be avoided by gently pressing down on the fabric.

3. Stick strips of adhesive tape along the sides of the card. Depending on the thickness of the rings that the silk is to be wrapped around, shorten the sides by about 1cm (½ in). Trim the end that is going to lie underneath the join right up to the edge of the card. The overlapping end also has adhesive tape on it and the overhanging silk should be trimmed away to allow you to peel back the protective film from the double-sided tape. Wrap the fabric tightly over the edge of the card and stick it down. Stick a second strip of adhesive tape on top.

4. Fix the card to both lampshade rings with clothes pegs. The ring with the support should be at the bottom and the other ring at the top. Try to position the welded joins underneath the overlap.

5. Gently peel the strip of adhesive tape away from its protective film bit by bit, and wrap the silk far enough round the ring so that it can no longer be seen. Do the same with the second ring. You must cut into the fabric a little bit to accomodate the crosspiece on the bottom ring. Finally, stick down the end of the shade.

Cushions

To make a cushion from your painted silk, 40 × 40cm square (16 × 16in), requires very little outlay other than the silk and a cushion pad. Two different techniques are shown here and both have seams worked from right to left.

Cushion with envelope opening

This method avoids the problem of inserting a zip fastener and involves using a little extra silk. The front of the cushion lies crossways to the length of the fabric.

You need painted silk 92 × 46cm (36½ × 18in), a cushion pad 40 × 40cm (16 × 16in) and matching sewing thread. Plan your design before painting the silk, so that the motif is shown centrally on the front of the cushion. The silk should not be too thin, otherwise the cover may have to be lined to stop the cushion pad showing through.

Method

- Turn one side selvedge under 2cm (½ in) and machine it, see diagram.
- Position the silk with the front side downwards, fold the shorter piece over, 20cm (7¾ in), with the longer one, 30cm (11¾ in) on top. Pin them together to form reverse side and machine 7–8cm (2½–3¼ in) on each side to form the opening, see diagram. Take care not to stitch the front as well!
- Pin the open side edges with right sides together, so that you can stitch over them with the machine about 1.5cm (⅝ in) from the edge of the silk. Trim the seam a little, slant the corners and turn the cushion cover to the wrong side, then stitch again 1.5cm (⅝ in) from the edge.
- Turn the cushion cover back on to the right side and iron the seams flat.

Cushion with zip opening

You need two pieces of silk 45 ×

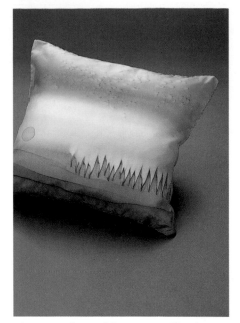

An attractive cushion cover will enhance any room.

46cm (17¾ × 18in), cushion pad 40cm square (16in square), sewing thread and a 30cm (11¾ in) long zip fastener.

Method

- Tidy up the bottom cut edges and mark the position of the zip.
- With right sides facing, stitch the bottom seam, using normal stitch length except for where the zip is positioned, when you should use a much longer stitch.
- Iron the seam flat. Sew the zip in by hand or machine. Undo the long stitches, opening up the seam by at least 10cm (4in), so that the cushion can be turned right side out.

  With the right sides of the front and back together, sew a 1.5cm (⅝ in) wide seam all round.

  Trim the seams and slant the corners.

  Turn the cushion cover to the wrong side and stitch the seams once again 1.5cm (⅝ in) from the edge.

  Turn the cushion to the right side and iron the seams.

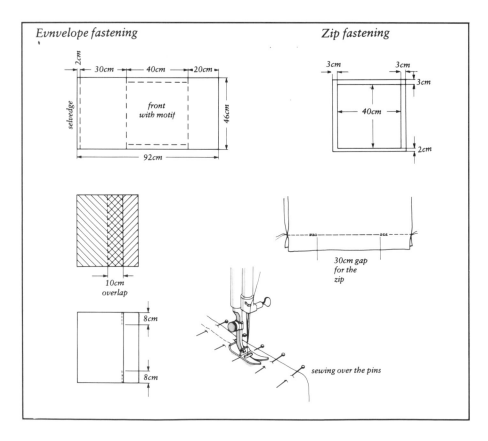

Evnvelope fastening

2cm
30cm — 40cm — 20cm
selvedge
front with motif
46cm
92cm

10cm overlap

8cm
8cm

Zip fastening

3cm   3cm
3cm
40cm
2cm

30cm gap for the zip

sewing over the pins

Skirt

This is simple and quick to make, as it consists of two straight pieces of silk. No shaping is required so when painting the silk you need not be restricted in your pattern. To allow the skirt to fall correctly, it must be cut across the line of the fabric, not on the cross. This means that the selvedges will be in the side seam stitching.

Take your hip measurements to work out how much material you will need but, generally, a total width of 140cm (55in) is sufficient. If the skirt needs to be wider, then you will have to paint the front and back separately. You will then need twice the length of the skirt, see diagram, but you may prefer a different length, according to your height.

A hand-painted skirt requires a pure silk lining which can be purchased in a suitable colour. If you wish to paint it to match the outer silk, use pongé No 8.

The outfit can be completed with a matching top or scarf. Make sure you obtain the same tones by mixing enough paint at the beginning.

Materials

- Crêpe de Chine, about 140 × 80cm (55 × 31½ in).
- Lining silk, about 140 × 75cm (55 × 27½ in).
- Matching thread.
- One wide, or 3 narrow waist lengths of elastic.

Method

- Fix the outer silk (and lining if hand painted), then wash and iron them. (If you are using 2 pieces for the circumference, sew them together using back stitch or machine stitch. Iron the seam flat.)
- Sew the outer fabric and the lining together, with right sides facing. Iron the seam.
- Join the side seam that is still open; take care to pin it on both sides so that the seams lie exactly on top of each other. Trim the seam.
- Turn the material right side out, with the stitching inside. Press the joins flat with an iron, about 5mm (¼ in) along the edge. When you insert the elastic, the side stitches of the lining round the waist need to be opened. Stitch one wide, or 3 narrow tunnels for the elastic round the waist, see diagram.
- Shorten the skirt and lining to the right length and complete the hem with a fine, hand-rolled seam.

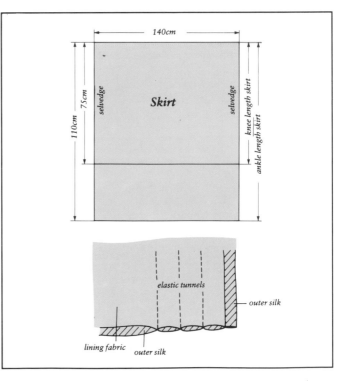

Sun top

Measure your bust to see whether the suggested amount of silk is sufficient and shorten or lengthen, as required. You will need about 55–60cm (21¾–23½ in), depending on whether you are going to make thin shoulder straps, or support the top with elastic.

Make a matching skirt, see page 85, and scarf, see page 89, to complete the ensemble.

Materials
– Crêpe de Chine, 55–60cm (21¾–23½ in) deep and 92cm (36in) long.
– Matching thread.
– Narrow elastic, if required.

Method
– Sew the side edges of the top together.
– Turn over the top edge and stitch it down.
– To make straps, paint 2 strips of material 45cm (17¾ in) long by 4cm (1½ in) wide. Sew the long edges together, to give a final width of 1cm (½ in). If using elastic, make a tunnel as given for the top of the skirt, see page 85.
– Hem the lower edge of the sun top.

Hints for making silk clothing
– Choose simple patterns. Large areas, such as skirts, offer more painting opportunities.
– Darts do often improve the fit of a garment, but they can also hamper the planning of the design.
– Harmonise the pattern, fabric and painting. Make sure you work out where the design should appear to best advantage; some parts of the pattern may disappear under folds.
– If you make a drawing of your proposed pattern, you can trace the outlines and try our various sketches for your design with coloured felt-tipped pens.

– Make sure the silk has been washed and ironed before transferring the design, see page 30.
– Transfer the pieces of pattern to the silk before it has been stretched out.
– The outlines of the pattern must remain straight after the silk has been stretched, so release any excessive tension of the material. Draw the outlines with an outlining agent.
– Always mix a sufficient amount of colour to complete the painting; you will not be able to repeat the exact tone later. The thicker the material, the more paint you need.

– Even if you only want to paint and steam-fix a small area of the garment, you should still put it all through the fixing process. White areas acquire a slight tint during fixing, and these stand out against unfixed silk.
– Steam-fixed paints are not suitable for painting garments which have already been sewn. The fabric cannot be rolled up for fixing without silk coming into contact with silk. However, small designs and motifs can be painted on to a ready-made garment, using a small embroidery frame so that you do not make holes in the fabric, with iron-fixed or chemical paints.

T-shirt

Whether you choose a graphic design, a flower motif or paint a landscape is up to you. What is important to note is that you should not begin to cut out the pieces until the painting and fixing have been completed, otherwise you will have problems stretching out the silk without distorting it. After fixing the silk, wash and iron it.

Materials
- To fit 16–18 bust, 130 × 92cm (52 × 36in) crêpe de Chine.
- Silk thread.

Method
- Transfer the pattern to paper, cut it out and lay it on the unstretched silk. The strips shown on the diagram are for trimming the neckline. Trace round the outlines with soft pencil, leaving an allowance of about 3cm (1¼ in). After stretching the silk, draw over the pencil lines with gutta. The front and back should have corresponding outlines.
- Cut out the pieces along the outlines.
- With right sides facing, pin the front and back together, then sew the shoulders, side and sleeve seams.
- Trim and press the seams.
- Before trimming the neckline, check that it is wide enough.

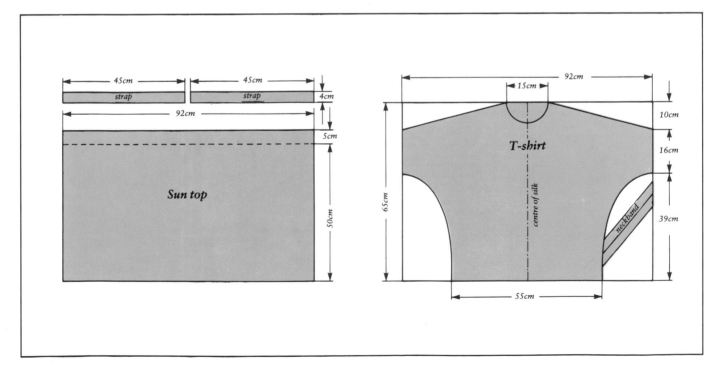

Long evening dress

This striking design is simple to make and easy to wear.

Materials

- Crêpe de Chine, or pongé 10, 120cm (48in) wide, by double your body length, measured from the shoulder to the ground.
- Waist length of elastic.
- Matching thread.

Method

- Cut the silk for the front and back and paint your design. Fix the fabric and wash it.
- Transfer the pattern to paper, lay it on the silk and cut it out.
- With right sides facing, join the shoulder and sleeve seams, trim and press the seams flat. Turn right side out.
- Join the side seams on the right side, from underarm to knee, see broken lines on diagram.
- Attach the elastic to the waist on the wrong side.
- Trim the outer edges and finish with a hand-rolled hem, or by machine.

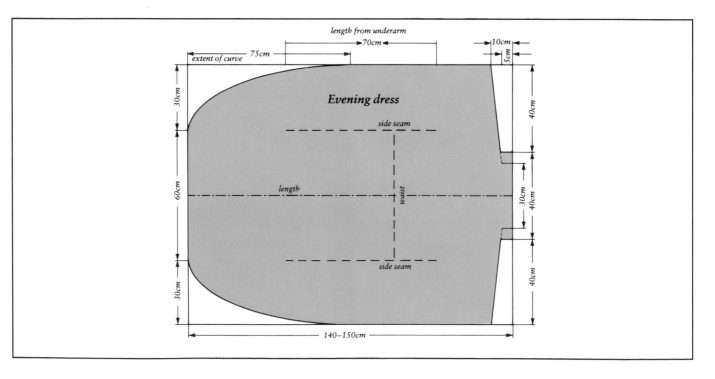

Scarves

The following pages will give you some ideas for painting silk scarves, without using preconceived patterns. The various techniques described on pages 41–61 were explored and many of the designs were produced through experiments. There are just two points to bear in mind; a scarf hangs in folds when it is worn, so it is not a good idea to paint a large, single motif which will not be seen to advantage, and a hand-painted silk scarf deserves a hand-rolled hem.

The design on the right shows tone-on-tone. The graphic framework of the pattern was drawn first with colourless gutta. The concentric circles in the design catch the eye, as they cut across the straight lines and are framed by the parallel stripes. Make sure that the gutta lines are not broken, so that you can fill in the areas in any order. Try to achieve as many layers of colour as possible, by mixing and thinning the paints.

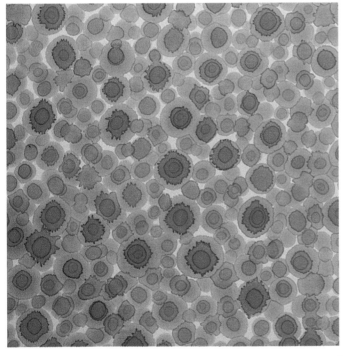

Experiment with spots of colour; place paint, water and alcohol next to each other and then on top of each other when the first ones have dried, until the whole area is evenly patterned, see page 46. By layering the colours in this way, dark focal points are produced, without having to add a different colour.

Paint the background with several colours and water, so that an even blending is created. After this has dried, begin in the middle of the scarf with gutta and draw straight lines to create a 'maze' effect. As soon as these lines are dry, brush on water, beginning at the centre.

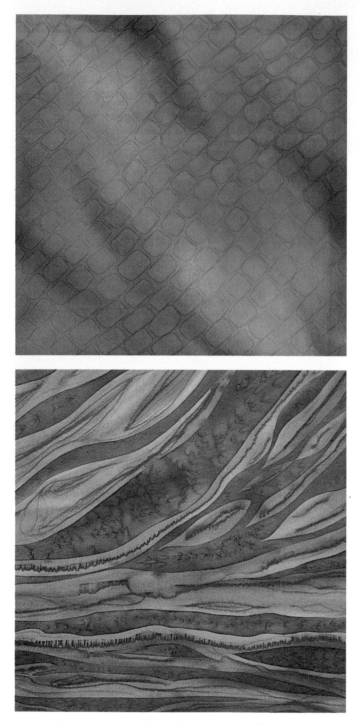

For the scarf on the left, begin by painting the background with a smooth flow of colours, or an area that has been brought alive by successive applications of mixed colours and water. As soon as everything is dry, use water and alcohol to create outlines, which are dried immediately with a hairdryer.

Hints on making scarves

The hem should preferably be hand-rolled but if you find this difficult, you can buy silk with a ready-rolled hem in the usual size for a scarf. There are disadvantages:-
— Marks from stretching remain visible on the hem, except when it is left white.
— The sewing threads do not always absorb the colour properly.
— The original square shape often becomes slightly rectangular after fixing and washing, particularly crêpe, and this cannot be corrected.

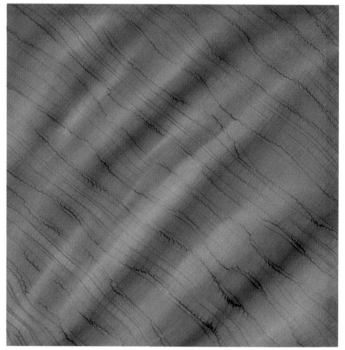

Paint the background with various colours, using a hairdryer to speed the process, so that a few contours are built up. When they are dry, enclose them with outlines of clear gutta. Paint the areas between and create salt effects.

Paint the background with blue-grey tones and water in diagonal stripes. When it is dry, draw in lines in the same direction with colourless gutta, making as many lines as possible next to each other. As soon as they are dry, draw stripes across them with water.

The design on the right is again dominated by diagonal lines. Prepare several colours for the first step, red, blue and two or three in-between tones. Begin in one corner and apply the colours quickly, one after the other, and blend them into the silk, see page 43. When everything is dry, draw lines with water in the other direction to the flow of the paint, so that contours are created. Leave to dry and then repeat the process, this time across the previous diagonal lines.

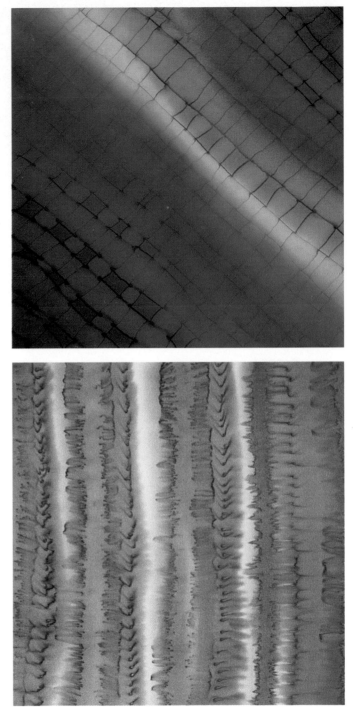

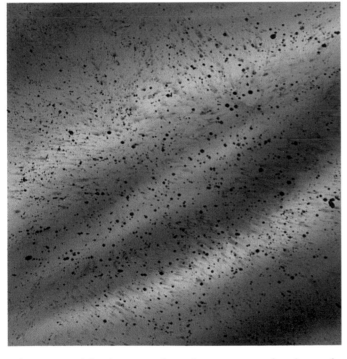

Alternate with water and various tones of colour, for example, a range of blue tones. Sprinkle concentrated colour on the silk while it is still slightly wet and repeat this when it is dry.

Place double rows of salt about 20cm (8in) apart and paint rows of colour between them, see page 51. When the paint is almost dry and the salt reaction has almost finished, place more double rows of salt in the spaces between.

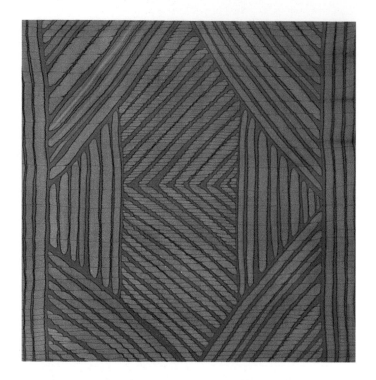

Concealed gutta, alcohol and just one mixed colour were used for this scarf. Parallel lines in all directions create the basic graphic design.

This design is reminiscent of waves. It was divided with gutta lines into thin, wavy stripes and painted with greys and pinks in varying degrees of brightness.

A Gallery of
Designs

Anne Emmerlich
Without title
24.5 × 18.5cm (9½ × 7½ in)
Twill

See page 93
Ahiraqué auf der Mauern
The space between day and dreams
8 × 8cm (3¼ × 3¼ in)
Honan and satin silk

Susanne Hahn
River landscape
28 × 20cm (11 × 7¾ in)
Pongé

Susanne Hahn
Embryo 1
80 × 80cm (31½ × 31½ in)
Pongé, padded silk

Susanne Hahn
Elmwood
85 × 85cm (33½ × 33½ in)
Pongé, padded silk

Susanne Hahn
Morning
from the cycle Melody of the day
80 × 80cm (31½ × 31½ in)
Pongé, padded silk

Susanne Hahn
Midday
from the cycle Melody of the day
80 × 80cm (31½ × 31½ in)
Pongé, padded silk

Susanne Hahn
Afternoon
from the cycle Melody of the day
80 × 80cm (31½ × 31½ in)
Pongé, padded silk

Susanne Hahn
Night
from the cycle Melody of the day
80 × 80cm (31½ × 31½ in)
Pongé, padded silk

Ilonka Zurbrüggen
Willow
50 × 60cm (19¾ × 23½ in)
Pongé

Ilonka Zurbrüggen
Birch
$60 \times 50cm$ $(23^{1}/_{2} \times 19^{3}/_{4}$ *in)*
Pongé

Heidemarie Schömig
Without title
40 × 42cm (15¾ × 16½ in)
Ponge

Heidemarie Schömig
Without title
40 × 42cm (15¾ × 16½ in)
Pongé

Heidemarie Schömig
Without title
40 × 42cm (15³/₄ × 16¹/₂ in)
Pongé

Heidemarie Schömig
Without title
40 × 42cm (15³/₄ × 16¹/₂ in)
Pongé

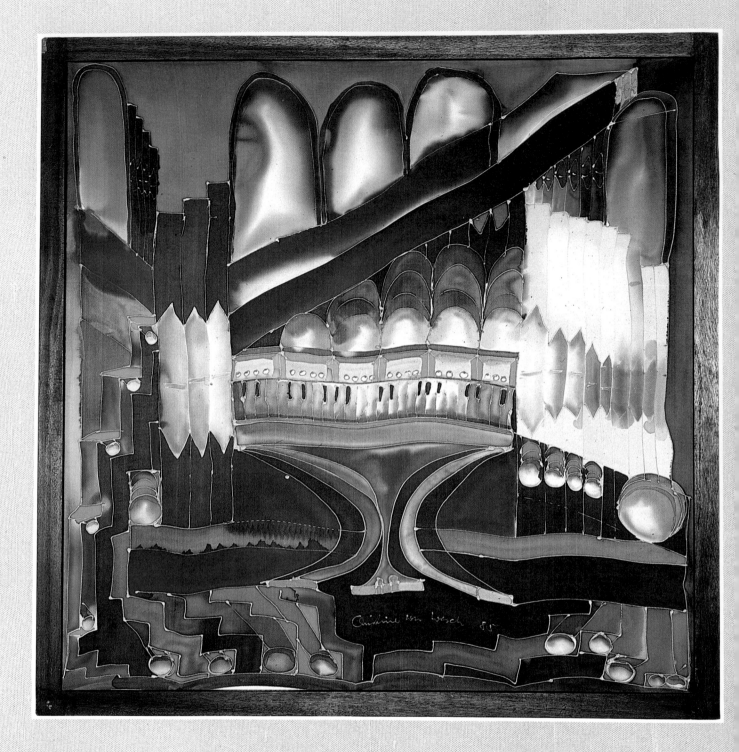

Christine von Loesch
Water music
92 × 92cm (36¼ × 36¼ in)
Crêpe de Chine

Christine von Leosch
The Hamburg Stock Exchange
92 × 92cm (36¼ × 36¼ in)
Crêpe de Chine

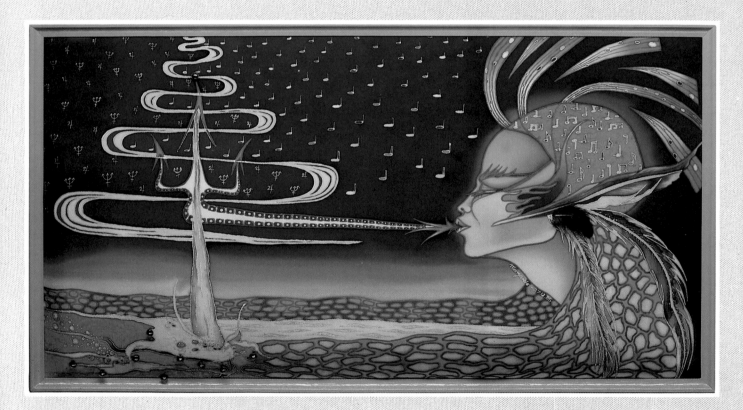

Margarete Schulz
Kosima II
90 × 47 cm (35½ × 18½ in)
Crêpe de Chine

Margarete Schulz
Nocturne
87 × 83cm (34¼ × 32¾ in)
Crêpe de Chine

Margarete Schulz
Eye communication
32 × 62cm (12½ × 24½ in)
Crêpe de Chine

Margarete Schulz
Aquatic plants
55 × 115cm (21¾ × 45¼ in)
Pongé

Margarete Schulz
Wanderlust
48 × 90cm (19 × 35½ in)
Pongé

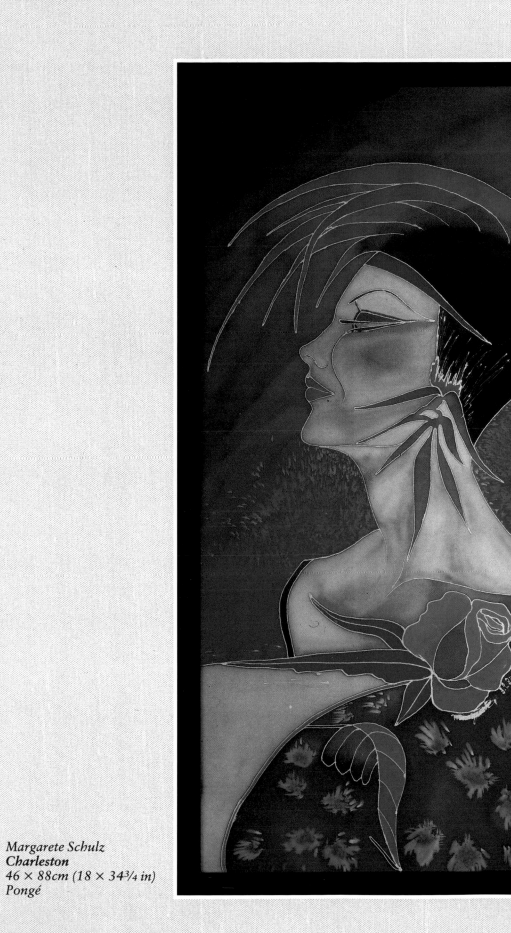

Margarete Schulz
Charleston
46 × 88cm (18 × 34³/₄ in)
Pongé

Margarete Schulz
Phoenix
90 × 90cm (35½ × 35½ in)
Pongé

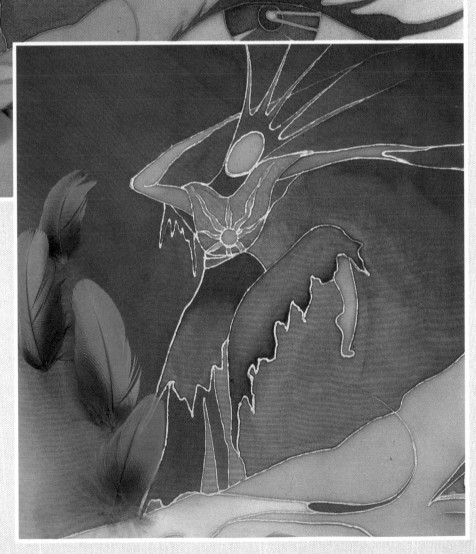

Two close-up details from the painting on page 112

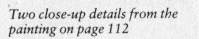

Ingrid Walter-Ammon
Mirage
41.5 × 45cm (16½ × 17¾ in)
Pongé

Ingrid Walter-Ammon
Awakening
68.5 × 61.5cm (27 × 24¼ in)
Pongé

Elke Franken
Forgotten?
29 × 36cm (11½ × 14¼ in)
Pongé

Elke Franken
Without title
35 × 39cm (13¾ × 15¼ in)
Satin silk

Ahiraque auf der Mauern
Rainbow night
22 × 25.5cm (8¾ × 10in)
Pongé

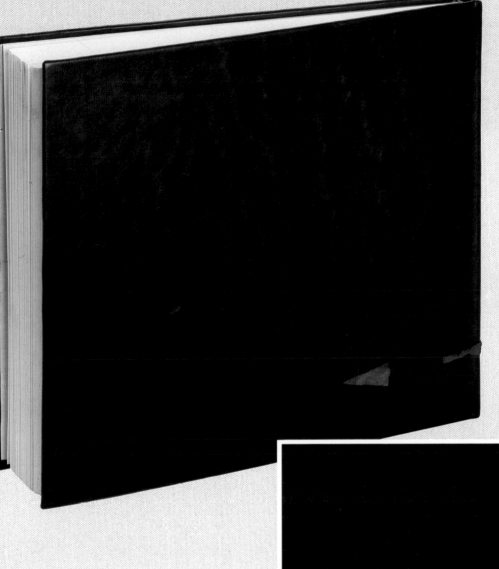

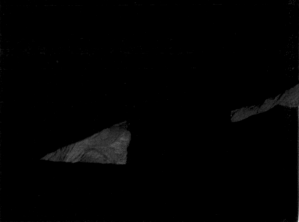

Showing the back of the book and a detail from it.

Clothing

A matching top was painted to go under this full, reversible jacket. The wonderful layers of colour and the casual style make it ideal to wear with jeans or silk trousers.

Rosemarie Breitbach
Satin, crêpe de Chine

An eye-catching combination of patterned top and plain trousers. The sleeves and waist of the top can be knotted to

In this ensemble, silk fabric and knitting have been combined.
The bright blue three-piece consists of a fabric skirt with a
ruched yoke, a pullover with silk sleeves, and a silk scarf to
complete the effect.

Karin von Ruville
Pongé, crêpe de Chine, knitting yarn

This design again features a
successful combination of
knitting and silk fabric. The front
shows a striking design but the
back has a marled effect.

Anne Emmerich
Front and back, satin crêpe, sides,
sleeves and waistband, wool and
silk with insets of angora.

*A stylish evening dress with a wrap-around skirt, a
bodice with a scalloped neckline, and full sleeves.
A matching belt completes the effect.*

Karen Coussa
Satin crêpe

This long, loose, full-sleeved dress allows an interesting
range of colours and shapes to be painted. Bold patterns
highlight the yoke and hem.

Ingrid Walter-Ammon
Crêpe de Chine

This gossamer overblouse is patterned in bright
yellow and black. It has a soft shawl collar and ties
with a simple knot at the waist.

Karin-Anna Arns
Crêpe georgette

The simple cut of this two-piece, in blues and greys, shows off the deliberately asymetrical design on one sleeve to good effect.

Ulrike Kniss-Sültrop

The knitted sleeves, welt and neckline of this pullover are
worked in black bouclé. An area of red adds contrast to the
geometric painting on the silk front and back, and a red trim
finishes the sleeves.

This T-shape silk blouse has elbow length sleeves and is boldly patterned. The effect is created with large and small areas of contrasting colours.

Susanne Hahn

This loose-cut jacket has batwing sleeves and is
fully lined. The beige and brown tones follow the
shape of the pattern.

Susanne Hahn
Crêpe de Chine

A flowing, waisted dress requires an extravagant amount of
fabric to achieve this romantic effect. It is painted in soft
yellows and has a silk lining.

Ingrid Walter-Ammon
Crêpe georgette

A combination of patterned and plain silk is used for this
softly waisted skirt, simple sun top and matching scarf.

Susanne Hahn
Pongé

Index

First published in Great Britain 1991
Search Press Limited,
Wellwood, North Farm Road,
Tunbridge Wells, Kent TN2 3DR
FIRST PUBLISHED IN PAPERBACK 1995
English translation copyright ©
Search Press Limited 1991

Translated by Daniel and Molly Lodge
Edited by Pam Dawson

Originally published in Germany by
Falken-Verlag GmbH
Copyright © Falken-Verlag 1987/1990
6272 Niedernhausen/Ts

Diagrams: Rolf Dähler, Bad Schwalbach

Photo agencies:
Abegg-Stiftung, Bern: p19, bottom.
Angemayer, Toni, Holzkirchen (Photo: Hans Pfletschinger): p20.
Blanke, Heinrich, Schlangenbad: p72–74.
Bruell, Susana, Herrenschwanden (Switzerland): p17 (silk houses).
European Commission for the Promotion of Silk, Düsseldorf: p18, 19
    top, 22, 23, 24.
German Textile Museum Krefeld: p15.
Franken, Elke, Constance: p116, 117.
Hahn, Susanne, Ludwigsau-Friedlos: p1, 41 bottom, 50, 52, 57 top, 58
    bottom, 59 top and bottom left, 69 top, 71, 81 top left and bottom
    right, 89–92, 96–99.
Kulturgeschichtliches Bildarchiv (Art history picture archive) Claus &
    Liselotte Hansmann, Stockdorf: p7 (Chinese painting: Lady with
    almond blossom. Indian ink and watercolour painting on silk.
    Unknown court painter. Yuan dynasty 1280–1368), p8–14, 16 top
    and left, 21.
Loesch, Christine von, Seevetal: p104. 105.
Pontoise Museums (Tavet and Pisarro), Pontoise: p16 bottom right.
Otto Maier Verlag (Publishers), Ravensburg, from: Johannes Itten 'The
    Art of Colour', p67 top.
Photo-Design Studio Gerhard Burock, Wiesbaden-Naurod: p2–5, 27, 29,
    31–33, 35, 36, 41 top, 42–49, 51, 53–56, 57 bottom, 58 top, 59
    bottom right, 60–66, 67 bottom, 68, 75–78, 80, 81 top right and
    bottom left, 82–88, 93–95, 106–115, 118–132.
© Quelle and Meyer Verlag Heidelberg, Wiesbaden, from:
    Krommenhoek/Sebus 'Biology in Pictures', p71 top left.
Schömig, Heidemaries, Hambach: p102, 103.
Zurbrüggen, Ilonka, Oelde: p100, 101.

The advice given in this book has been carefully selected and tested by the author and original publisher. However no guarantees can be given. The author, the publisher and their representatives cannot be held liable for personal injury, damage to property or possessions.

If you have any difficulty in obtaining any of the equipment mentioned in this book, or are interested in any art and craft titles published by Search Press, please send for advice or a free catalogue to: Search Press Ltd., Dept B, Wellwood, North Farm Road, Tunbridge Wells, Kent, TN2 3DR.

The publishers would like to thank the Silk Association of Great Britain for their help in editing this book.

ISBN 0 85532 720 0 (C)
ISBN 0 85532 718 9 (Pb)

Composition by Genesis Typesetting, Laser Quay, Rochester, Kent
Printed in Malaysia

If you are interested in any other art and craft titles published by Search Press, then please send for a free colour catalogue to:

Search Press Ltd
Department B,
Wellwood, North Farm Road, Tunbridge Wells,
Kent TN2 3DR, England
Tel: (01892) 510850   Fax: (01892) 515903

or (if resident in the USA) to:
Arthur Schwartz & Co., Inc,
234 Meads Mountain Road, Woodstock, NY 12498
Tel: (914) 679 4024   Fax: (914) 679 4093
Orders, toll-free: 800 669 9080

OTHER SILK PAINTING BOOKS PUBLISHED BY SEARCH PRESS

If you are looking for an exciting hobby, try painting on silk. The results are stunning and unusual – no other material can produce such luminous colours. The techniques are simple and with a little 'know-how' and a bit of patience, stunning items can be created for the home, for gifts or for fashion wear:

The Art of Painting on Silk
Volume 1
Edited by Pam Dawson

This book describes the basic techniques, tools and materials, required to paint on silk, followed by colourful examples of designs and finished items that will be useful to both the beginner and experienced artist. Useful motifs to trace are given in the final section of the book.

The Art of Painting on Silk
Volume 2 – Soft Furnishings
Edited by Pam Dawson

A colourful and inspirational book which covers a wide range of soft furnishing designs, from cushions and wall hangings to bed covers and lampshades. Each design is shown in full colour together with details of materials required, methods used and simple to follow charts of the painted motifs.

The Art of Painting on Silk
Volume 3 – Fashions
Edited by Pam Dawson

Volume three in the silk painting series gives plenty of practical advice on how to apply designs to stunning silk fashion garments. The book is full of colourful illustrations showing scarves, blouses, jackets, childrens' and babies' wear and a beautiful wedding dress, each with its own charted design.

The Art of Painting on Silk
Volume 4 – Potpourri
Edited by Pam Dawson

Simple and more complex designs are colourfully illustrated and accompanied by easy-to-follow charts showing motifs for greetings cards, wall hangings, shawls, scarves, lavender bags, cushions, accessories, neckties and paintings.

How to Paint on Silk
Edited by Pam Dawson

Abridged edition of The Art of Painting on Silk: Volume One.

Create beautiful gifts with this simple and colourful guide to painting on silk; greetings cards, brooches, cushions, pictures and scarves.

Painting Flowers on Silk
Daisies, roses, irises, poppies and convolvulus
Lydie Ottelart

This stunning and practical book is for silk painters who want to develop their skill and produce innovative floral designs. The book begins with an important and useful section on how to draw flowers and includes many floral motifs which can easily be traced. The author illustrates unusual techniques, such as hot wax, stencilling and sugar syrup methods, and using colour, silver or gold guttas and watercolours are also illustrated. There are colour illustrations of finished items such as cushions, scarves, paintings, tablecloths and a nightgown.

Inspirational Silk Painting from Nature
Renate Henge

This book will be a source of inspiration to silk painters who wish to create their own original designs. Beginning with a reminder of the various techniques which can be used in silk painting, there follows a gallery of full colour photographs from nature and examples of finished silk paintings. Subjects covered include the sea and sky, landscapes, trees, fruit and vegetables.